What Is Left

My Less-Than-Graceful Journey on Kilimanjaro

Florian Eizaguirre

To my parents,
For teaching me to choose the hardest path,
And for giving me the confidence that I could handle it

CONTENTS

PROLOGUE

I felt dizzy. How could I feel dizzy lying down? The sun radiated through the orange walls of my tent. The walls became an incandescent yellow. With no airflow, the heat quickly rose inside. Every inch of my skin felt moist, and I suddenly became aware that I hadn't showered in a week. I considered getting out, but my head was now pounding so hard that my ears started ringing. The heat was the least of my worries. My whole body was screaming in distress, and I didn't know how to help it. I wanted to throw up but couldn't afford to lose the small quantity of food I had just managed to ingest. I wanted to breathe fresh air on a slow stroll, but any movement made all my neurons fire up with pain. I had no experience to compare this to. It was not the satisfying exhaustion felt after a tough workout. It was more like a desperate call for it all to stop, a call for the animal brain to take over and run away.

Was Lahara right? As our lead guide, he had seen hundreds of people going up Kilimanjaro, and he knew who had made it to the top and who hadn't. Maybe going back down was my only option. Maybe this was as far up this infernal mountain as I was supposed to go. It was hard to tell, hard to think. How much more torture could my body endure before shutting down? A seemingly simple yet life-threatening question I had to answer.

By now, I had lost track of the reasons for my decrepit state: physical exhaustion, mental exhaustion, dehydration, lack of oxygen, lack of nutrients, lack of quality sleep ... Lack of common sense, most of all.

In contrast to the invisible chaos wreaking havoc inside me, the walls of the tent were completely still. How could there not be wind this high up the mountain? Focus, Florian. You can't procrastinate. It is not going to get easier.

I looked at my watch. 6:45 p.m. Lahara had just announced that the group would start hiking at 10:30 p.m. I tried to remember some of the reasons why we were summiting at night, in the hope of finding a loophole. First, summit day was by far the longest of the trip, so we had to start early: it was an eleven-hour hike to the summit and back to base camp, and then another couple of hours to make it down to an even lower camp. Then, it was apparently hard to sleep at such high altitude—the human body was not meant to be so high in the sky—so we wanted to spend as little time there as possible. And all the water we needed from here on was carried up by porters from streams far below. Unfortunately, these all seemed like legitimate reasons ... That left me with only three hours to sleep. How was a three-hour nap supposed to magically put my body back together, enough so that I could make it to the summit? It beat me.

At least I knew one thing for sure: my body was not adjusting fast enough to the high altitude, and it would not get better until I went down. Not everyone made it to the summit. There was no shame in calling it a day. Maybe it was time to grow up and make a sensible decision for once in my life. Maybe it was time to give up.

I had promised myself I would if it got too tough.

A CONTENTIOUS DECISION

It had made so much sense two weeks earlier.

A major project at work was finally coming to an end. For the past two years, working as a management consultant, I had been traveling back and forth virtually every week between Chicago, where I used to live, and the Bay Area, where my clients resided. For two years, the novelty of traveling for work and the laughable pride of achieving the highest loyalty status with major airlines and hotel chains had managed to hide a feeling I could not ignore anymore: I had walked the thin line between happily busy and burned-out for too long. My recent move to Portland, Oregon, an effort to shorten my time in the air, had done little to help. It was time to take some much-needed time off.

One evening, from my hotel room, I started my typical modus operandi when planning a vacation. Step 1: Look at a map of the world and find a country that piques my curiosity. Step 2: Do a quick search on the culture and top activities to validate that the trip will be exciting and photo worthy. Step 3: If affordable, book a plane ticket and a hostel for the first night, and figure out the rest on the ground.

This time felt different, though. For two reasons. First, I felt self-imposed pressure to outdo my previous trip to South Korea, during which I had checked the box not only on a new country but also on a whole new continent. Over an intense four days, I had walked through Seoul in search of glimpses of all major temples, markets, and parks, and even sneaked in an afternoon in the demilitarized zone between North Korea and South Korea. The mad rush had culminated in a picture of me standing on the Freedom Bridge at the border between the two Koreas; I posted the photo with the cheesy hashtag #seoulsearching. Mission accomplished. I had been to Asia, my sixth continent. I had visited yet another country. According to the posts on my Instagram account, I had clearly outgrown my French passport and should be promoted to a "global citizen" who deserved global citizenship credentials. The facts that I hadn't really taken the time to experience Korea and that I had gone back to work more tired than when I had left didn't seem to matter.

Someone judgmental would say that I was having a quarter-life crisis, and that this was more of an escape from reality than a nurturing, meaningful vacation. They would be right. After having skimmed through over thirty countries and not remembering much of anything, I felt deep in my bones that it was time for a change. I needed to do more than just tick a box, more than create a just-another-day-in-my-life post on social media (I am not exaggerating: check out my first-ever Instagram post and the shameful caption "Just another Sunday in Venezuela").

There was a second, scarier reason why this time was different. A new sense of urgency was being continuously fed by everyone around me. "Enjoy your freedom while it lasts," "Life as you know it is about to end," "Sleep while you still can," and the occasional "This is the most beautiful thing that will ever happen to you." Fearful and hopeful, I was counting the months before my wife, Celeste, would give birth to our first baby. Seven months to go. So far, the most troublesome task had been choosing a name. We had one for a girl: Clarke. But we hadn't reached a consensus on a boy's name yet. Boy or girl, this was likely the last vacation I would be taking without the constraints and joys of little humans for a very long time. I had to make it count. The question now was: Where to go?

Vietnam? I could eat my way through Hanoi's street-food scene, rent a motorcycle and explore the backcountry in search of rice fields nested in deep green valleys, and finally reward myself by cruising Halong Bay. Or should I go to Belize? I could scuba dive in the Blue Hole and embark on a quick escapade to Guatemala to visit the Mayan ruin of Tikal, hidden in the rain forest. I could easily imagine what all of these trips would be like: pack a small backpack, race to see as many things as possible, hop from hostel to hostel. I would travel without seeing, come back exhausted on a Sunday night, and curse myself as I logged on at work the following morning. Somehow, I did not feel the adrenaline rush that usually comes with exploring trip options. I knew it was a privilege to be able to travel. But I could not find any meaningful criteria to help me decide where to go.

A novel idea popped into my mind: Should I have a staycation for the first time in my life? It sounded healthier. But how could I tell my family and friends that I had decided to adopt a sedentary life before fatherhood forced me into it? Who was I without reckless adventures? A boring, mature grown-up? It felt like giving up. On the other hand, going to Vietnam and Belize felt like running away.

Looking absently at the top Google results for "miraculous one-week trips that will give meaning to your life" in hope of finding a quick answer, my mind drifted to the last time I felt truly content on vacation. The memory was not hard to summon. It was two years ago. I was completing a three-week hike through the Pyrenees mountains between France and Spain. I had never walked more than a couple of hours before, and making the mountains my temporary home for weeks had been life-changing.

I remembered how hard the first couple of days had been. I remembered how sore my legs had been. Especially when I would wake up and have to start hiking again. The first few steps before my body warmed up had been so painful that I grimaced in despair. I remembered thinking halfway through the first day, "These mountains are gorgeous, and I love being outdoors, but do I really have twenty more days of this?" And yet, after a couple of days, on the other side of pain and frantic boredom, my internal clock had slowed down. My focus had shifted to the present moment, and for once, I didn't have any act to perform. In the present, I had found contentment. Going back to civilization, busy and crowded, had been hard but for the right reasons.

I realized that there had been no shortcuts. And now, there would be no shortcuts either.

I knew then, deep in my gut, that hiking was the answer that would get me out of my Cornelian dilemma. Walking toward a goal rather than running away from "real life." Sweating my stress away instead of worsening it by chasing after a chaotic schedule. Almost immediately, my intuition whispered, "Kilimanjaro." As I contemplated this thought, the picture became clearer and clearer. Kilimanjaro was shrouded in a mystical aura, prone to helping anyone disconnect from the modern world. Towering at 19,341 feet above sea level, it was the highest freestanding mountain in the world and the tallest mountain in Africa, making it one of the Seven Summits (the tallest mountains from each continent) and a worthy challenge. Most importantly, there would be no cell signal or WiFi on this dormant volcano, so I wouldn't be tempted to check work emails or scroll absentmindedly through social media posts. I finally felt excitement rising and started doing some quick homework.

Kilimanjaro could be climbed in a week. Check.

Kilimanjaro could be climbed by anyone who was reasonably fit. Check. Kind of.

The price tag was pretty high but could be decreased by choosing a short, seven-day hike. Check.

There were still open spots for the coming week. Check.

And as luck would have it, with the seven-day option, I would be summiting on my father's birthday. I am a notoriously bad gift giver. Well, after years of being a disappointment, I finally had a unique, meaningful gift.

I stopped long enough to wonder if climbing Kilimanjaro was dangerous. A quick search confirmed that "climbing Kilimanjaro is probably one of the most dangerous things you will ever do." Another morbid search revealed that the reported number of deaths among climbers was "only" ten fatalities per year. The risk seemed acceptable. I decided to discount my fear.

With this thorough ten-minute preparation done and boiling with excitement, I decided that I couldn't wait to fly back from the Bay Area to Portland at the end of the week to tell Celeste in person. I had to call her now to share the great news.

"I finally decided where I am going next week," I announced, and paused for a couple of seconds to build up the suspense. "I am going to Tanzania to climb Mount Kilimanjaro!"

Celeste was no stranger to adventures and travels herself. She was born in Pennsylvania, had spent two years in a small community in the Dominican Republic as a kid, grew up in Santa Fe, New Mexico, and like any self-respecting travel aficionado, she had opted for an international exchange in college and spent a year in Puebla, Mexico.

The two of us had met in Buenos Aires, Argentina. She was doing an internship at a prominent female-owned graphic design firm. I was doing my self-respecting travel aficionado exchange semester at the Universidad de Buenos Aires. And after I'd put in three long months of tedious labor, my French accent finally convinced her to become my girlfriend. We celebrated by taking our first trip together to Iguazu Falls, a gorgeous string of waterfalls nested in the jungle at the border between Brazil and Argentina. During that trip, I saw Celeste take a close-up picture of a huge tarantula and climb up a liana higher than I was comfortable going myself (and she threw a final blow at my shame by hanging upside down at the top). That was when I both fell in love with her and got permanently scared of her. To this day, she maintains that the tarantula was dead, but, even if it was presumably dead, no one entirely sane would have gotten their camera lens so close that it was tickling the killer animal's hair.

After eight years together and countless adventures abroad, Celeste was used to hearing me throw out extravagant ideas to see what stuck. She had come to expect them, and she had not only perfected the art of handling them skillfully, but she had also fully accepted her role as the lifeguard who reeled me back in when I couldn't see reality, my needs, or my abilities clearly. This would be one of the first times that I would travel abroad alone since we met, so her job was all the more important now.

"It sounds exciting and intense! Don't you need to train for it?"

"Well, I have a week. I read that anyone reasonably fit can

climb it."

"And you feel you are reasonably fit?"

"Maybe," I answered.

Celeste stayed silent. She trusted that even I could see the gigantic holes in my reasoning.

"Almost no one dies climbing Kilimanjaro. I will be OK." I realized too late that revealing my search about my chances of not making it out alive did not convey the confidence I was trying to assert.

"It seems risky, considering you've done no preparation …" I could hear concern in her voice.

"I have designed a very rigorous workout plan for this week," I lied. "I'll be ready by the time I board my flight."

"I am not sure what a week will change. Have you asked Paul what he thinks about it?" Paul was a friend who loved hiking and had just climbed Kilimanjaro. I remembered seeing pictures of him training with a medical crew. He was on a stationary bike, an oxygen mask covering his nose and mouth. A massive tube connected the mask to a large, white, expensive-looking medical device. The whole setup was supposed to simulate the lack of oxygen the body is exposed to on Kilimanjaro, but given the diameter of the tube, it could as well have been used to feed him whole steaks at regular intervals. The bottom line was that Paul fell squarely in the category of rational people who trained seriously and knew what they were doing before adventuring on Kilimanjaro. "I haven't had a chance to connect with him yet, but I am very confident I can make it. Aaaand, I'll be summiting on my dad's birthday! How cool is that?"

In the silence that followed, I could picture Celeste weighing her concerns for me against my pressing need for a meaningful trip.

"Well, I am not sure how excited your family will be,

knowing that you're going without much training. To be honest, I am a bit worried, so I imagine that they will be stressed out— and justifiably so." I worried about where she was going next. "But if you think a week is enough ..."

I made a mental note to reassure everyone, but a conditional agreement was all I needed: my idea was potentially aligned to reality. I booked the seven-day climb. I had a goal. I had meaning. Now I just needed to train.

That's when the complications started.

CHANCE FAVORS THE PREPARED MIND, TOO BAD

While everyone online agreed that virtually anyone could attempt Kilimanjaro, all the testimonies of training plans I found included six months to two years of intense strength and cardio training, culminating in climbing all the Colorado 14,000 footers with a fifty-pound backpack. Far from getting dispirited, I chose workouts adapted to my fitness level to fill my week: two strength workouts, a couple of light runs, and a stroll up Mt. Tabor, the tallest local hill in Portland, sitting at a proud 636 feet above water. I was hoping that this busy schedule would at least make my body realize that it needed to get moving. I only had seven days. I was determined to make every single one of them count, and then I'd rest on the twenty-hour plane ride. All the dots were quickly connecting. This trip was so much more than a refreshing, energizing break. This was supposed to be the start of a new, active, balanced life for me. I was supposed to get back in shape for good, after years of carelessness. This workout plan was only the beginning. I could feel it in my bones: I was going to turn my physical health around for good. Starting right now.

The next day, I got the flu.

I almost never get sick. The only times I do become sick are when I am about to go on vacation, as if once my body detects an imminent break, it releases all the stress and denied emotions that have accumulated since the last vacation. The result is a glorious concerto of signals, ranging from fatigue to irritability, that seems to shut down my immune system. The disease almost always manifests as a light cold. This disquieting flu was new. For a week, I could barely get out of bed, as if the flu had spent thirty years plotting against me and had waited to strike at the exact moment it could ruin my life. By the day before I was supposed to take off, the only physical conditioning I had done was my daily morning sit-up to get out of bed and drag myself out of the bedroom.

Physically and mentally exhausted, I finally decided to put aside my stubborn, blind optimism, and I called Paul for advice. I tried to ignore his chuckles as I walked him through my predicament. I shared all of it. The burnout. My strong need for a healthy escape. My questionable fitness level. My tight deadline for making a decision. And my newfound companion, the flu.

"Oh, Kilimanjaro! It's really an amazing experience!" Paul started in an encouraging tone. "As far as training goes, you do need to be in good shape to make it to the top. To be honest, I am not sure you'll make it in your state. I didn't train for Kili since I run almost every day, but I did do a hypoxia test to simulate the conditions at the summit and check how my body reacted to the lack of oxygen. I seemed to handle it well, so I didn't even end up taking Diamox."

I thought back to my own accidental test with high altitude. It had occurred a decade earlier on Aconcagua, the highest mountain in the Americas at an elevation of 22,837 feet. I was traveling with a Czech friend, Torv, and we had decided to visit Mendoza, the wine capital of Argentina, to celebrate the Fiesta Nacional de la Vendimia, aka The Grape Harvest National

Festival. One evening, after sampling most of the wines produced in the region, Torv had the astute idea of going on a day hike on Aconcagua the next morning. We didn't let the fact that we were both hungover stop us, and took a bus to a random trailhead on the mountain. I realized that, surprisingly, I wasn't the less prepared of the two when, after an hour of walking, Torv asked me if I had toilet paper.

"No, sorry, I barely remembered to bring water," I replied, genuinely sorry that I couldn't help.

After soldiering through the pressure for another thirty minutes, Torv finally called for a break and headed down toward a stream to take care of business.

"I am not proud of it," he announced after coming back up, "but I had to leave my underwear behind."

"You gotta do what you gotta do. I just hope the chafing won't be too bad." His pants looked really rough all of a sudden.

An hour later, it was my turn to call for a break. I started feeling so dizzy that I could not walk straight, and my vision began to get blurry. Torv quickly identified the symptoms as altitude sickness and warned me that things would get a lot worse for me if we kept going. He mentioned conditions like pulmonary edema and cerebral edema, which sounded pretty serious, and as I would later learn, are indeed life-threatening. We rushed back to the trailhead and took a bus to the nearest health center, where Torv's diagnosis was quickly confirmed. I was given a pill and ordered to go back to a lower altitude. By the time we were back in town, at lower altitude, all symptoms had disappeared.

I snapped back into the present and wondered if I should share that I had not passed my own hypoxia test with flying colors. But then I decided against advertising a pattern of questionable decisions. "How dangerous is Kilimanjaro?

Really."

"The only real danger I'd worry about is altitude sickness. Other than that, it is not a technical hike. If you are sure-footed and comfortable with heights, you'll be fine." I thought I was sure-footed enough, and I didn't remember ever being afraid of heights, but my standards were probably not Paul's standards. He was an accomplished mountaineer who hiked every weekend. I was an accomplished workaholic who Netflixed every weekend.

"If you were in my shoes, would you get on that plane tomorrow?" I asked, not knowing if I really wanted to hear his answer.

"If I were you, I'd reschedule. Chances are you won't make it to the top in your state, and seeing the summit is what it's all about. And this is a serious investment of time and money, so I don't know if you'll go back anytime soon and try again." The ring of truth in his voice was quieted by my emotional impulse to go somewhere, to do something, anything.

"I don't know if I can reschedule. Everything is already booked—my time off, the plane, the trip ..." We were both engineers by training, so I decided to stick to hard statistics. "If I go, what are the chances of me making it to the top and the chances of me making it out alive?"

"As I said, you mainly need to worry about altitude sickness. You'll get plenty of warning before you drop dead, so just listen to your body. If your head is hurting, turn around. If you are nauseous, turn around. If you have issues breathing, turn around. As far as making it to the top, I'd say your chances are pretty slim ..."

If I had to summarize, going on this trip was not a smart decision, but my chances of failure were not exactly 100 percent, and I would probably live if I listened to my body. I still didn't fully understand how dangerous Kilimanjaro really was, but Paul's answers were all I needed. The risk seemed manageable. And if I didn't come out alive, it would make a funny tombstone: "He was not that smart, but his chances of failure were not quite 100 percent, so he gave it a shot. At least he died with his underwear on."

The next day, my fabulous headache and I boarded the plane to Moshi, Tanzania.

NEW FEELINGS AND LIFELONG MISTAKES

Celeste likes to joke that one of my superpowers is to fall asleep before a plane takes off and to wake up when it touches down. Which makes for great trips for me but long and silent ones for her. Two hours into the first leg of my long trip to Tanzania, it became apparent that my undesired viral companion was my kryptonite. Eyes closed, head gently resting on the palm of my hand, upper body supported against the aircraft window, blind down, I had everything I needed to fall fast asleep, but my acute headache was sending pain signals throughout my body, just often enough to prevent me from even dozing off. A feeling I had never experienced in an airplane took an increasingly strong hold: boredom. My legs started to get restless. My neighbor felt very close. The person in front of me was reclining just a little too far. I felt trapped. I got annoyed. Then angry. Then got distracted by a throbbing headache long enough to forget my anger. And as soon as the surge of pain stopped, the cycle started all over again.

I wondered if I should open the letter Celeste had given me before I left. She had explicitly instructed me not to open it until I was climbing Mount Kilimanjaro, but the prospect of temporary relief from my hell loop made it hard to abide. She would never know … Unlike me, Celeste was a great gift giver. Something to do with her being able to put herself in the shoes of others. I had never fully grasped the concept. The letter would probably be a great source of motivation and a confidence booster when I would need to start trudging up steep slopes. Surprising myself, I decided not to open it.

Twenty hours later, at nighttime, I landed in Moshi, my sanity hanging by a stretched thread. I had become religious somewhere over the Mediterranean Sea after a torturously wakeful layover in Amsterdam, and my fervent prayers for a bed were finally close to being fulfilled. I could not get out of the plane fast enough. I rushed through the small terminal to the baggage claim and waited as close to the beginning of the conveyor belt as possible. I was playing a fairy tale over and over in my head: As luck would have it, my bag would be the first one to come out, I'd find my driver right away, and after a short ride to the hotel, the receptionist would have my keys ready to be picked up as I entered the lobby. The story culminated in a glorious picture of me entering my room to find a comfy bed and an unlimited supply of aspirin sitting on the nightstand.

Miraculously, my bag was indeed one of the first to come out. I made a mental note to keep up my newfound religious practice. Prayers did work. I proceeded to the exit and started the slow, awkward walk, reading through all the signs held up with companies' and people's names. I quickly found my driver and went to introduce myself.

"Welcome to Tanzania!" he greeted me, with more energy and enthusiasm than someone should legally be allowed to display in front of tired long-distance travelers. "My name is George. We are only waiting for two more guests, and we'll be on our way." He must have seen in my eyes the fairy tale fading away, as he added with a reassuring smile, "Their plane got delayed, but they should be here any minute now." Any minute became thirty minutes, then an hour. As I vowed to go back to my miracle-less atheism and considered taking a nap on the hard concrete, the two guests finally decided to show up. The ride to the hotel was a blur. In the night, I vaguely noticed the two-lane highway, the rudimentary median dirt strip separating us from the sparse oncoming traffic, the few small towns scattered amid what looked mostly like farmland, and the dirt roads branching off into the dark.

As we got closer to Moshi, houses got closer together, sidewalks became concrete, and we met more traffic despite the late hour. Our van slowed down as the highway merged into a large roundabout with a ten-foot Kilimanjaro replica at its center. We must have entered the town itself, as concrete buildings started to mushroom around the dimly lit streets. Some of the buildings did not look finished, but no construction seemed ongoing.

We quickly arrived at our hotel and pulled off on the side of the road. A security guard in full uniform slid open a massive black iron gate when he saw our van. George thanked him, and we entered a paved compound. We drove past a couple of white buildings of different sizes and parked in front of the tallest one, a four-story building with large balconies sticking out.

George handed us our bags and led us to the hotel lobby. Over the past three years, I had spent more nights in hotels than in my own home. Hotels had come to be familiar, but this one left me perplexed. It was as if the hotel was trying to be luxurious, but details betrayed another reality. The lobby was spacious, but the furniture looked old. The ceiling had numerous lights, but only one was on, barely providing enough light to fill out our arrival form. It was hot, but there was no AC, which was noticeable coming from the AC-loving United States.

After checking in, a hotel employee dressed all in brown walked me to my room. Past the lobby, a large section of the back wall was open to a backyard lit by moonlight. Outside, we were greeted by tall palm trees. The air was hot and humid, making me feel like I was sweating. To our right, a large staircase swirled up to the floors above. We took a left and walked past a long swimming pool, toward one of the smaller buildings.

The glorious moment I had been dreaming about since landing was finally here. I was finally about to rest. My room was on the ground level. I opened the door to find two single beds and a small bathroom. It was everything I needed. I closed the curtains, threw my bags on one of the beds, dropped a white mosquito net hanging from the ceiling around the second bed, and unceremoniously passed out.

I woke up refreshed and was hopeful that I had finally gone through a couple of restoring deep sleep and REM cycles. I looked at my phone. 3:18 a.m. My body had graciously allowed me a full three-hour reprieve. On the bright side, I thought, lying inside my protective white-net cocoon, that hopefully meant that I'd have no issues falling asleep early in the evening and would quickly adjust to the new time zone.

This morning was my only chance to explore Moshi, so I got up and headed out as soon as it was light out. The security guard at the gate nodded as I approached. He looked like he wanted to engage but stayed quiet, and I wondered if he spoke English. I considered making my go-to joke that "English is not my mother tongue, as my stereotypically thick French accent indicates," but I remembered just in time that I wasn't in the United States anymore and held off. A lot of people around here probably had accents too. I wasn't special anymore.

"Do you know where I can find an ATM to withdraw money?" I risked, rubbing my thumb over the tips of my index and middle fingers, hoping that it was a universal gesture for money. The guard pointed to the right, a confident smile on his face. I thanked him and walked out of a side gate, emerging on a main road used by a few cars and a lot of motorcycles. The "sidewalk" was, I imagined, the space between the weary asphalt road and the hotel fence. It consisted of an uneven dirt path sprinkled with large flat rocks and gravel, and was ornamented with ankle-breaking potholes that kept your attention focused on where you adventured with your feet. It was a quiet early morning; no one else was walking outside. Across the road to the left was a huge park, also protected by a tall fence. Enclosed on all sides and with little view of the surroundings, I realized that this street was probably not meant for pedestrians. Far ahead, past this claustrophobia-inducing block, under a bright blue sky bothered only by a few white clouds, I could see colorful buildings and people walking around. I kept moving toward this scene of daily city life.

Down the road, a huge five-story gated mall was already busy, despite all of the lights inside seemingly being off. I found myself perplexed again. From outside, the building looked modern, with an appealing architectural style that explored various round shapes and tall, dark blue windows against an off-white concrete structure. But inside, the dimly lit space and the still escalator made me wonder if the place was shut down, despite the activity swarming around me. I walked past an open convenience store with narrow aisles and found the ATM. I withdrew enough Tanzanian shillings for my morning escapade and started wandering indolently through town.

On a side street, a lively group of locals outside a cafe caught my attention. I headed toward them and into the cafe for my first authentic Tanzanian experience. I ordered an espresso and pointed to a pastry I had never seen before, a peculiar mix of a muffin and a croissant. The waitress, who had greeted me in English when I entered, stayed silent after I gave my order and pointed me toward the tables. I wished I had learned the basics of Swahili but decided to blame my lack of preparation on the flu. It was easier than accepting that I was lazy.

I sat outside to soak up the energy from the group and the surroundings. Across the street, several colorful kiosks were displaying various items for sale, from clothing and shoes to pineapples and opened watermelons that gleamed red in the sun. Nature was embedded in the town; tall trees randomly took over the sidewalks with no apparent planning. It was like the town had been built on top of the existing vegetation instead of completely taking it over.

Passersby were wearing a mix of clothing, from jeans and T-shirts to more colorful traditional dresses and tunics. Several men were wearing the iconic red *shuka* that, based on my reading on the interminable plane ride, I identified as a Maasai cloth. A woman in a green-and-blue dress was carrying a large basket on her head. People weren't walking head down, frantically scrolling through their phones, oblivious to the world around them. They were here, present. Just as I had this thought, I realized that actually, several people were on their phones, scrolling. I was seeing and noticing what I was expecting: Africans who live at a slower pace, undisturbed by the ravages that technology wrought on our attention span. But of course, smartphones had made their way here, too. Realizing my biased filter, I started seeing more and more people on their phones. The waitress interrupted my powerful train of thought to bring my order. Oh, if she only knew how much more woke I was now compared to when I ordered …

I drank the espresso in one draft, gobbled my breakfast, and continued to explore Moshi. I was hoping to find a local newspaper in English to get a feel for what was currently important and of interest to people here. As I often do when I am in a new place, I stopped at every cafe on the way in search of day-to-day life scenes—yes, I was lurking. One of the cafes had its catchphrase, "Onja Mlima," written on its walls and chairs. The waiter explained that it translated into "Taste the Mountain" and referred to the extensive coffee plantations cultivated in the fertile volcanic soil on the lower slopes of Kilimanjaro.

Five cafes and five coffees later, I was wired but still hadn't found a newspaper. The sugar rush from the couple of pastries I had devoured was starting to morph into a sugar crash, and I decided to head back to the hotel. I hoped to sneak in another quick nap before meeting with my guides and my group at noon.

On the way back, I was painfully reminded that Moshi was less than 250 miles from the equator: I had completely underestimated how much more powerful the sun rays were here. As anyone with a bit of common sense would have anticipated, the combination of heat and caffeine was the perfect recipe for a headache. As my head started throbbing, I realized that just when I had finally gotten rid of my flu-induced headache, I had managed the impressive feat of replacing it right away with a new one. The saddest part was that I had no regrets. Well … I wished that by now, I had learned that a cup of water between coffees helps, but I found it acceptable to suffer for my impromptu, haphazard vagabonding style.

I made it back to my room with enough time for a quick shower and a power nap, but the caffeine running through my veins had other plans. Instead of napping, I ended up making a long mental list of everything I would do differently the next time I decided to take on a 19,000-foot mountain, starting with packing a barrel of melatonin to sleep at will.

A LAST CHECK AND A LAST COMFORT

At noon, I headed to the lobby with my large duffle bag fully packed, as instructed. After booking the trip, I had received a comprehensive packing list with everything I would need on the mountain. It contained obvious hiking gear: from light to warm clothing, sunglasses, a first aid kit. And also some worrying items like earplugs, because "snoring travels well in quiet camps," and wet wipes, because "staying clean is a challenge."

George was already in the lobby, talking to two fellow hikers, Fiona and Rama. After quick introductions, we jumped in an old van and headed out to the hiking company's headquarters on the other side of town. Back home, lying comfortably on my couch, it had been easy to think that I could handle Kilimanjaro. Now that the rubber had hit the road, despite my blind confidence still being by far the loudest voice in my head, I felt the urge to compare myself with Fiona and Rama. I wouldn't let the fact that I knew almost nothing about them stand in my way.

Fiona came from Australia. Tall, blond, with an easy smile that made you want to be her friend. Her confident stance and the quality of her gear, which had clearly been tested and proven in the wild, made her look like a serious hiker. The only thing I thought I had going for me by comparison was age. She was probably in her fifties, and I had just turned thirty. Yes, she was in shape, she had the experience, she had the gear, and she knew how to use it, but I was confident that I would live forever and could do anything until proven otherwise.

Rama, on the other hand, was more of an enigma. He was from India. He was short—well, he was my height—and he seemed to be only as fit as I was. So far, I had gathered that he was a chemical engineer, living at his company's compound. He had answered the couple of questions I had asked as if he wanted to say more, or say something different. As if I wasn't asking quite the right questions.

"How did you prepare for Kili?" I couldn't help but ask them both over the loud engine.

Rama had the same look on his face, as if he was figuring out the best answer to this slightly wrong question.

"I did a lot of stair workouts over the past six months," Fiona answered. "Both with and without a heavy backpack on. I also did a lot of long hikes. And last year, I did Everest Base Camp to make sure I could handle the altitude."

"Nice! How was Everest Base Camp? Would you recommend it?" I asked, partially out of genuine interest and partly to hide my self-conscious focus on everyone else's fitness level.

"I would. Some people complain about the trash on the path, but I loved it anyway. It is a special place on Earth, and seeing Everest was amazing." I nodded and turned to Rama.

"I am used to walking in the mountains. Every year, I go to Ladakh in the mountains north of India."

"How is the hiking there?"

"I go there more as a retreat. To draw and to think."

I nodded again. "I always wanted to do a meditation retreat in the Tibetan Himalayas," I said and immediately regretted it.

It reminded me of how annoyed I get when I say I am French and someone answers, "Oh, I went to visit Italy during my undergrad!" Not the same, man, not the same.

Instead of looking annoyed, Rama smiled, the way an adult smiles at a child who is discovering something obvious while not fully understanding it. It was not a pretentious smile, but more like a considerate one.

I sat back in my seat as we entered a large open field surrounded by high walls. Immediately to our left was a small building that looked like someone's house. It was the size of a one-bedroom, with no signs or distinctive features outside of the iron bars protecting the windows. The house was dwarfed by the rest of the property, which consisted of around 40,000 square feet of flat ground, covered by green grass that had been walked on so much that mud puddles appeared in some places. It was used as a staging area for excursions to Kilimanjaro. Everywhere, staff was busy cleaning gear, drying clothes, folding tents, and packing large, colorful duffle bags tied together with elastic rope. Further to the right, some more staff was sitting at a table, arguing and planning in lively voices.

We parked by the house, and as we came out of the van, three people came to greet us. Lahara, Daudi, and Thomas would be our guides for the next seven days. Their main task, or so I hoped, would be to keep us all alive.

They directed us to an empty table outside. A large brown tarp had been spread on the ground right next to it. We all sat down, hikers on one side of the table, guides on the other. Lahara, our lead guide, walked us through what to expect on Kilimanjaro and shared tips to make the climb as pleasant as possible, from "Drink before you're thirsty" to "Invest in our portable toilet option."

Lahara, Daudi, and Thomas were all from the Kilimanjaro

area, which was comforting. I had chosen this company because it advertised itself as being Tanzanian owned and operated, employing locals and paying them a decent wage. The guides were all very different. Lahara was Maasai—one of the two main ethnic groups in the region, along with the Chaga—and was by far the tallest of the three. He was bald and, as expected of someone who regularly ran marathons, slender. His measured demeanor made him look wise beyond his years. Daudi was the most relatable: average height, average build, average appearance. He seemed more reserved, speaking few words and speaking them softly, but making them all sound supremely important. Thomas was the youngest, just a bit shorter than Lahara and quite muscular. He made me think about the kind of person who doesn't seem to eat particularly well or work out that often, yet is always fit and always high energy.

Once they answered all our questions, it was time to review the gear we had brought, to make sure that no one would realize at the top of Kilimanjaro that they didn't have warm socks and that their toes had turned purple. Fiona, Rama, and I started unpacking our duffle bags on the tarp. I took out my coconut-flavored chocolate bars. I took out my chocolate-flavored chocolate bars. As I took out my chocolate-covered nuts, I looked over and realized that Fiona and Rama were only laying down clothes and gear. That made sense. I wondered if I should explain that, being French, chocolate was more of a first aid kit item than a luxury snack that porters would have to carry up the mountain. And after all, when else would I eat these guilt-free if not while hiking a 19,341-foot volcano?

"Rama, do you have any gloves that are warmer than these?" Daudi asked, raising an eyebrow.

"No, but these ones are good," Rama answered, seemingly not noticing the concern in Daudi's voice.

"They aren't warm enough for the summit. It gets really cold and windy up there."

"I use these gloves when I go to the mountains. I'll be fine," Rama replied, serenely confident.

"What about pants?" Daudi tried. "Do you have anything warmer than these sweatpants? For the summit."

"No." Rama was smiling almost apologetically now. "But these will be enough for the summit."

The three guides looked at each other. "We really recommend that you at least rent a pair of long warm underwear, Rama. It's not fun, walking in the snow freezing after hours of hiking."

Rama's face betrayed the battle gently raging inside of him. He obviously thought that he had brought everything he'd need on Kilimanjaro. He finally gave in to appease Daudi: "OK, I'll rent a pair of long underwear." I couldn't tell if Rama was a natural mountain man who didn't suffer from cold temperatures, or if he was delusional and wouldn't make it one day on the mountain.

I gladly agreed to rent the recommended long warm underwear, despite having brought ski pants for summit day. I still hadn't been able to shake off my headaches or my soreness and didn't need to add "shaking uncontrollably because of the cold" to the already long list of obstacles on my way to the summit: over-caffeinated body, joyous virus taking its sweet time to leave the premises, high levels of abdominal fat … From now on, I was going to make responsible decisions. Better late than never.

Fiona went last. She had nothing to rent.

We were all directed to the small house. It was used as the company's headquarters and consisted of a main living room with couches and all sorts of maps on the walls, a small room with the gear for rent, and a small office where we were sent one by one to pay cash for the remainder of the expedition fee.

"Get plenty of rest tonight" was Lahara's parting advice. As his eyes scanned the three of us, I could have sworn that they stopped on me longer than they should have.

That night, lying in my bed, reality started to hit. This was my last night in a proper bed for a week. It felt so comfortable, as if I were hiding from the physical effort to come. Well, it would be the last night for a week in a proper bed only if I made it to the top and didn't give up early. Which would be devastating, and potentially humiliating, but at least I would have a comfortable bed again.

This prompted another realization: I had the privilege of being at the feet of Kilimanjaro, at the border of Kenya and Tanzania. I thought about my parents in France, my sister in London, and Celeste in the US. I sent a last message on Eizaguirre Land, a family group text that included all of them. "Hopefully I'll message back in seven days!" Creating peer pressure had always been an effective source of motivation for me.

I put my phone away and closed my eyes. Starting tomorrow morning, there would be nowhere to hide.

FREE AS A MONKEY, AT LAST

Our climb got delayed by bureaucracy. Every porter entering Mount Kilimanjaro National Park was required to check in and weigh their bags to make sure that they weren't over the limit of twenty kg. per person. A noble policy, but one that caused long waits just as the excitement to get started was building up. Without cell service to kill time on smartphones, a large group of hikers accumulated under a rudimentary shelter, and lively discussions filled the air. Fiona, Rama, and I met the remaining four members of our team, who had arrived late the previous night: Younes, Fred, Hughes, and Raoul.

Younes was a fellow Frenchman in his thirties, but the similarities between us stopped there. He was a wellness and fitness coach from Lyon, and looked like a model straight from a magazine. Chiseled biceps, sharp jaw, trendy haircut, brand-new gear that fit perfectly. He hadn't trained for Kilimanjaro either, or rather, he had not trained for Kilimanjaro specifically, but his excuse was better than mine: he works out for hours every day; it is his job.

Fred, from Canada, was a hardcore athlete. He ran ultramarathons, long Spartan races, ironmans, and other shenanigans that would require me to have four more lungs and a couple of spare legs to compete in. He also ran to work every day because, unlike common wisdom would have it, it was more convenient than driving. His thick beard and extensive tattoos made it hard to believe that he was in his early twenties, a good ten years younger than any one of us.

Hughes and Raoul also came from Canada. Hughes was in his early thirties and Raoul early forties. They were hardened travelers. Tanzania was just one of the stops along the way on their epic two-month adventure throughout Africa. They had come to Moshi to climb Mount Meru a couple of days earlier, in order to acclimatize to high altitude before attempting Mount Kilimanjaro. Despite living in the shadow of the tallest peak in Africa, Mount Meru had nothing to be embarrassed about. It stood at a height of 14,980 feet, and making it to the top was no small feat. Hughes and Raoul were born storytellers. Their recollection of climbing Mount Meru seemed straight out of a Tolkien novel and included missed windows for the final push to the summit because of dangerous weather, parched biscuits for their only sustenance during an eight-hour hike, and a beat-up jeep racing down a steep, winding rocky path.

We were discussing one of Fred's crazy races involving swimming in a frozen Lake Tahoe when Thomas called us. All the paperwork was sorted out, and we were ready to start walking. This was it. After a week of overthinking and under-doing, this was showtime. I gave a last look down toward the Chaga villages, the multitudes of banana trees, and the coffee farms we had just driven by on the lower slopes of Kilimanjaro, then faced forward and walked through Machame Gate.

We had finally entered Mount Kilimanjaro National Park.

Walking felt liberating. Stuck under the shelter, I had been painfully aware of how weary my whole body felt after a week of being sick, topped with an accumulating lack of quality sleep and a lasting jet lag. Past Machame Gate, we had immediately been greeted by towering, moss-covered trees. The wide dirt path we were on crisscrossed through a dense rain forest. Tall sycamore trees with gray-brown camouflage bark offered a perfect playground for all sorts of vegetation to grow, from a fluffy, dangling moss called "old man's beard" to massive ivy plants forming triangles from the ground and up the trunks. The green forest floor was so dense with tree ferns, tall grasses, and bushes that we could not take a single step off the path without having to stop and assess where to step next. The trees above had been shedding enough to create a thin mat of yellow leaves on the path, which kept our hiking boots from getting too muddy.

Countless birds could be heard. I peered up, searching through the trees and the gaps in the canopy of green and brown, but I couldn't find any. The temperature was perfect for hiking, and the gentle slope was a great warm-up. Lahara was leading the way at a leisurely pace, and since I was only carrying my day pack, it felt like I could walk like this forever. It was all going to be OK. My body relaxed, and my mind slowed down, matching the lazy movement of the branches rocked by the wind, and leaving behind the hectic rhythm of urban life. My thoughts drifted away.

And were quickly brought back to reality by a commotion high in the trees. I looked up just in time to see five monkeys gracefully jump the fifteen feet across the road. The monkeys were black, save for their white faces and the white strip along their backs and tails. They didn't pay any attention to us. They clearly had places to be. One by one, they jumped, spreading all four limbs, and landed heavily on thin branches that swung dangerously low before settling back to their original position.

This forest was full of life, and so was I.

"These are white monkeys," Daudi informed us.

"I hadn't realized we would be walking in a gorgeous forest," I said. "Most of the pictures I saw of Kilimanjaro were a lot rockier."

"Kilimanjaro has five climates, and we'll go through all of them. This rain forest is only the second climate. Don't worry, it will get rockier and rockier," he answered with a smile.

Everything around us was very different from the various landscapes I had gone through in the Pyrenees. The luxury of having guides and porters was also very different from hiking alone and carrying everything needed to survive for weeks. I was grateful for the help, since I needed it, but I missed the quiet, introspective headspace I had found in the Pyrenees. I was wondering what I would get out of this new experience when Younes caught up with me.

"Do you live in Lyon?" I asked him, pointing to the clean Lyon soccer jersey he was wearing.

"Yes. Huge fan of the Olympique Lyonnais. How about you? Marseille?" he asked, smiling at my thick Southern French accent.

"Close. I'm from a small town next to Montpellier." I smiled back. "Always great to hear that even after living in the United States for ten years, I still haven't lost the accent."

"Definitely haven't lost it! I can feel the sun on my face when you speak. And picture people relaxing on a beach, drinking pastis," he added, referring to a high-proof spirit that tastes like anise and that had become very popular in Southern France.

I wondered if it would take too long or be too pretentious to explain that I had become a workaholic in the United States, and that I didn't recognize myself in my native region description anymore. Even at the bottom of remote Kilimanjaro, no one could escape stereotypes.

"So, what brings a fitness coach from Lyon to Kilimanjaro?"

"The thrill of challenge, I guess. I do a lot of short and explosive workouts, and I am comfortable with that. I wanted to test if my body and mind could sustain a longer effort."

All I could hear was "if." If this guy wasn't sure he would make it, what was I even doing here? But his "why" really resonated with me. I understood the need for a good challenge. It was also part of why I was here, I thought.

Kilimanjaro was the thrill of challenge.

"And then there are my girls," he continued. "I have three daughters. I am hoping that this adventure will teach them to dream big and to take on exciting challenges."

"Great lesson to teach by example! I'll take notes, since I will join you in the fatherhood club in a couple of months." I noticed that I was relating to a young parent for the first time in my life. "I am happy to see that having kids does not stop you from traveling and going on adventures. I was thinking this might be my last one for a long time."

"This is actually the first time I've left them for so long," Younes answered with an apologetic smile. "It was a hard decision to make, but I realized that I had to accomplish everything I am meant to accomplish if I am to become my best self and the best father I can be." Younes was speaking my language now. Self-development had always been one of my obsessions, and I liked the way he saw growth as a person and a father. "I did buy a satellite phone to call them and my wife every day. And to be available in case of emergencies." I made a mental note of it: I would need to be more organized as a father if I was to go on solo adventures.

I pointed with my chin to his new-looking shoes. "Did you break them in?"

"First time wearing them! It is actually my first time hiking, so everything on me is new, except for the jersey." He nodded at my purple hiking poles. "I didn't know they made these for men."

I looked at him, and his smile grew even larger. Teasing was also my favorite way to connect with people, so I let go of the slight sexism and laughed liberally. It was on. We kept bonding back and forth for a while.

A WALKING PARADOX

As the path climbed steadily upward, the trees thinned and got smaller. Painted wooden signs nailed on trunks indicated the names of the trees we were walking by. At a tree called "Podocarpus falcatus, East African yellowwood," we took a cutoff to the right that ended on a large alpine field. Thomas, who had walked ahead with the porters, greeted us at the entrance of Machame Camp. Despite our late start, we had made it with daylight to spare. Hundreds of small, colorful tents had mushroomed on all the flat spots. The camp was swarming with activity. Some porters were carrying big buckets of water; some were relaxing and chatting in circles. Some people were cooking. Some were cleaning.

Thomas led us to a cluster of orange tents, our mobile homes for a week, and introduced us to Ashim, our camp manager. Ashim would be our go-to person for anything we needed when not hiking. To make it easy on us to find him, he was tall and wore a bright neon-blue jacket with bright red sweatpants. He showed us which tent was whose and where to find water to refill our empty bottles. "Dinner is in ten minutes in the big tent there," he finally announced, pointing to a relatively large blue tent nearby.

I opened my tent to find my duffle bag lying beside a thick foam "bed" that looked heavenly after a day of hiking in the forest. I pushed away all thoughts of trying it out, not trusting myself not to fall asleep. I changed out of my hiking boots and made my way to the blue tent.

In the Pyrenees, dinners were always a joyous affair. After a long day of hiking and a cold lunch, eating hot soup was something to look forward to. Yes, it consisted mainly of ramen noodles, but the luxury of having something warm in the wild was all that mattered. And now, without fail, when our cook, William, brought us food, it was warm. The only two differences were that the food he brought tasted like it was freshly made (because it was), and that it was part of a deliciously elaborate four-course meal including soup, chicken, veggies, pasta, and dessert. William wore an olive-green jacket and a dark blue bandanna on his head. He did not speak English, but his enthusiastic nods and the way he described every dish he brought with a one-word description made us feel like he was communicating with us just the same. He seemed to appreciate the awe in our eyes as he and Gabi, who was assisting him, brought in plate after plate. Most of dinner was spent talking about how amazing it was to be served such quality food 9,840 feet high.

After dinner, Lahara introduced us to the health check routine we would perform every evening on the mountain. A disparate array of data would be collected, from a very accurate and scientific measure of our blood oxygen levels, to the highly subjective answer to the question, "How are you feeling on a scale from 0 to 10?"

"This is a pulse oximeter," Lahara said, holding out a device that had a surprisingly fancy name for something that looked like a large clothespin clipped on his forefinger. "It measures our blood oxygen levels. At sea level, your blood oxygen saturation would be close to a hundred percent, but here, it will get lower and lower as we start climbing up. On the mountain, anything above ninety percent is good. High eighties are OK." The pulse oximeter used light beams to measure how much oxygen was being carried by our red blood cells, compared to the optimum capacity. My understanding was that, since our fingers are far from the heart, if they were well oxygenated, the rest of our body was also doing well.

The oximeter made its way around the table. Rama's finger was 96 percent oxygenated. Younes's finger was at 97 percent. I never had great cardiovascular capacities. As Celeste liked to tease, if I had been cast in *The Lord of the Rings*, I would have been Gimli, the dwarf, not Legolas, the elf. I could carry weighty objects and break things, but my heavy bones would have a hard time running fast longer than thirty minutes. I started taking deep breaths as the oximeter got closer, hoping to send every extra oxygen molecule available to my laboring red cells. When my turn came, I clipped the device on my finger and waited for the screen to give its verdict. 99 percent. I could barely believe it; my underwhelming pulmonary system was not exposed just yet. I turned to my health tracker and proudly wrote 99 percent before jumping on to the next questions. The "How are you feeling?" question received an optimistic 9. Headaches? Yes, but not from the altitude, so I wrote, "No." Loss of appetite? Not yet. Vomiting? Not yet. Diarrhea? Not yet … Were they really expecting us to get that busy on the mountain?

Once we were all done, we looked at each other's answers. I was glad to defy logic: I had the highest oxygen levels, and yet I was supposedly the one feeling the worst. My generous 9 was falling short of the resplendent 10s of Hughes, Fiona, and Younes, and of the worthy 9.5s of Raoul and Rama.

I decided not to overthink it and went to bed, confident. We had just climbed 4,000 feet, the most we'd need to climb in a single day outside of summit day, and it had proved easy. Today had been a great day.

WHEN A HUNGRY TEAM BANDS TOGETHER

I woke up to the familiar ring of my cell phone alarm clock. My body and mind were automatically getting ready for the daily professional grind, until I realized that I was on Kilimanjaro and I would not be looking at any spreadsheets today. But I barely relaxed; the damage was done. My familiar headache also woke up. The same headache that had been with me at the hotel, on the plane ride, and back at home. It liked me too much for my taste. Stress and pain, two uninvited guests taking their sweet, sweet time to leave the premises. At least, my body felt much stronger than it had since I got the flu. Hopefully, this was the light at the end of the tunnel.

I needed to change my ringtone. Something more ethereal, something fit for the endeavor at hand.

"Wash, wash!" came a surprisingly energetic voice just outside the tent. I put on shorts and a sweater and came out to see what was so exciting this early in the morning. I was greeted by a large basin and a young crew member who looked like today was the best day of his life. He was shorter than me and wore an apron. "This is warm water to wash. I am Gabi, and I am helping around camp. If you need anything, you can ask me."

Some people love their jobs, and everyone around them can tell. Gabi loved his job. He was happy on the mountain. He was happy helping hikers to adjust. He reminded me that life is simple when we pay attention to and are grateful for small day-to-day pleasures.

I thanked him and made a mental note to ask him his secret for bright-and-early overwhelming bliss. Around us, the camp was slowly waking up. I looked around to make sure that I was not about to break the basic rules of human decency. After finding several hikers outside splashing generous amounts of water on their bodies, I undressed down to my underwear in the frigid, damp morning and rinsed off as fast as I could. Every hair on my body straightened in a valiant but vain effort to protect me against the cold, my invisible assailant. Despite the shivers, the hot "shower" felt heavenly, considering that we were already high on the mountain and that there were no modern amenities around.

By the time I joined the group in the blue tent, food and drinks were already served. Everyone was helping themselves to coffee, tea, bread, cheese, and, quite randomly I thought, cucumbers. After our rich dinner, I had wondered if breakfast would be equally extravagant. But this simple menu was to be expected and would do great. As I tried to temper my excitement, William walked in with a large plate filled with dozens of flatbreads, some folded in triangles and some rolled. They looked freshly cooked, gleaming with oil, promisingly warm, and deliciously sweet.

"Looks like French crepes!" I drooled as my sugar addiction took over, and I leaned forward. "What are these?" I asked, pointing at the welcomed sweets.

"Chapati," William answered, visibly enjoying our excitement. "Chapati."

We dived in, and the verdict was unanimous: chapatis are delicious.

After breakfast, we got ready for the day's hike and left our tents and heavy bags behind. When we arrived at Shira Camp this afternoon, our tents would already be set up.

The forest looked different, illuminated by the morning light. Many shades of green and brown were competing for our attention. My eyes were drawn to the bright, light green, my favorite color in the thin canopy above us.

As we made our way out of Machame Camp, we discovered that we had stopped right at the edge of the forest. The tree line revealed magnificent views under a cloudless sky. Below and behind us, the dark green forest was spreading as far as we could see, all the way down the gently rolling hills at the bottom slopes of Kilimanjaro. And in front of us, not too far in the distance, there it was. The snowcapped summit of Kilimanjaro. The sun was beaming to the east, almost right behind the summit, reflecting on the snow and forcing us to squint against the brightness of the sky. I couldn't help but smile. It wasn't that high. It wasn't that far.

The muddy trail took us from the protective forest, full of life, to an exposed landscape of shrubs. As if the mountain wanted to remind us that serious business was only beginning, the trail quickly got steeper, forcing us to look down at our feet to navigate around the boulders along the path. Shoulder-high evergreen trees lined the winding trail. Now and then, huge boulders became the only path up, and we had to spread our arms to keep our balance. Flowing around us, porters were easily making their way up, carrying heavy bags on their backs or on their heads. Or both. Some had flips-flops on. Others wore worn sneakers. We were all wearing hiking boots, but between the stumbling and walking on all fours, our comfort level on these rocks was debatable. I couldn't imagine having to deal with constantly clenching my toes to keep the flip-flops attached to my feet.

The air changed. It got colder. Murkier. We were now in the clouds.

Daudi announced a break.

"We should take a selfie," Younes proposed. He had been taking a lot of pictures and videos on his GoPro since Machame Gate. Sometimes, he documented the landscapes we were going through. Other times, he spoke to his daughters, explaining what he was thinking and feeling.

Younes took a telescopic stick out of his day pack and attached it to his GoPro. All these accessories were making his bag a lot heavier than mine, but Younes didn't seem bothered. We all gathered and took a picture, accompanied by the sound of a boring "cheeeese."

"Should we choose a team name to cheer us up?" Younes suggested. Everyone loved the idea and started throwing out predictable names. The A-Team? The Dream Team?

Finally, Fiona jumped in with a strong candidate. "Team Chapati?" We had it. Everyone quickly agreed, and, where seconds ago stood seven strangers walking up a mountain, now stood a close-knit team of fellow climbers united around the common goal of reaching the top of Mount Kilimanjaro.

We took another selfie, screaming "Chapatiii!" which earned us the smiles of porters passing by. There is nothing like a group of adults shouting "pancakes" in public to brighten the day.

WONDERS

"Great find on our team name," I congratulated Fiona as we hiked deeper into Kilimanjaro's third climate, the heath and moorland. It looked like the Scottish Highlands on steroids: taller, browner, and wilder. Human-sized scrubby shrubs and tall half-sphere grasses were everywhere against the light brown rocky soil. The path was now wide enough and friendly enough to allow for casual conversations.

"I live in a small village close to Melbourne," Fiona shared. "When my kids moved out to the city, I started looking for a pastime to stay active. I found hiking, and it became a passion."

"Funny how life works." I chuckled. "Here we are, far from home on this remote mountain. You because your kids left the house. Me because mine is on the way." I paused for a moment. "I was looking for a meaningful break before becoming a dad. I think that coming here was the right choice. I haven't slowed down like this in a long time."

Up the path, some porters were stopping at the bottom of a fifteen-foot waterfall to fill up their bottles. I imagined the water was coming from the snow at the top of the mountain, melting under the powerful sun. Fiona and I walked around the quiet pond the waterfall had created and jumped over the small stream continuing its way downhill. The porters from our group waved, and we returned their greetings.

"It is hard not to be present and take things in when you are surrounded by all of this," Fiona agreed. "And at the same time, the physical challenge keeps you focused." Fiona was right. I looked ahead and took in the moment.

Kilimanjaro was being fully present and focused. One mountain. One goal.

By early afternoon, we entered Shira Camp. Nested at a respectable altitude of 12,600 feet, Shira Camp was located at the edge of a gigantic plateau that was ended abruptly by a sheer cliff. Our tents had been erected a safe distance from the dangerous fall on barren dark earth. Human-sized boulders were scattered around camp. A permanent bathroom was sitting on the other side of the tents, at the edge of a grove of short trees growing on a mat of tall yellow grasses. Some courageous ravens were investigating the camp, maybe in search of food discarded by hikers.

Lahara announced that we were finally going to be introduced to the whole crew that had been helping us from the beginning. I wondered why we hadn't met the team yet and realized that the first day had been busy, from checking in at the Park to making it to camp at nightfall. We all met outside, and one by one, everyone introduced themselves. Besides Lahara, Daudi, Thomas, Ashim, William, and the ever-smiling Gabi, eighteen other porters completed our band. Introductions ended with catchy singing, dancing, and laughter.

"For those of you who have a lot of energy left, you can do an acclimation walk to the top of this hill," Lahara mentioned once the group scattered. As I considered his offer, my body made it clear: I am drained, go take a nap. I obliged, and after a power nap, I emerged back out to the world of the living.

From my tent, I saw the silhouettes of Hughes and Raoul against the dimming sky. They were standing at the edge of a cliff, watching the horizon. As I got closer, I realized why they were petrified there. The view was absolutely breathtaking, almost otherworldly. We were right above an endless sea of clouds that came crashing on the cliff in a frozen white whirlwind, going up high toward the cosmos. I looked up, tracing the clouds, only to find another layer of clouds above us. In between, we could see Mount Meru, which Hughes and Raoul had climbed just days earlier.

I could not take my eyes off the lights and pirouetting clouds in front of us, but ended up breaking the deep silence to get back to more earthly concerns. "My wife is a photographer," I shared. "She would love to capture this marvel." I turned to Hughes and Raoul. "Do you guys have significant others?"

They looked at each other with knowing smiles. "We're married."

It took me a moment to realize what they meant. They had not shown any act of affection toward each other since I had met them. "Sorry, I hadn't realized!"

"Good. Same-sex marriage is illegal in Tanzania, so we are not advertising it."

As we headed back to camp for dinner, Raoul reminisced about their hike on Mount Meru until he remembered an important detail. "I hope that we will have a decent meal before attempting the summit and not just munch on dry biscuits like we did on Meru." His tone told me that I had better eat a lot before summit night.

That night, everyone scored in the mid-nineties on our blood oxygen tests. Our guides were satisfied and left us with some parting thoughts. "Tomorrow, we are going up to 15,000 feet before going back down to camp. It will be a critical day to adapt to high altitude."

For the first time in a long time, I felt a childish excitement take over. I was just about done beating the flu. "Tomorrow is the day I get over the bump and start fully enjoying this adventure," I thought.

TO EAT OR NOT TO EAT

We settled into our routine. Wake up. Wash, wash. Breakfast. Walk. Eat. Health check. Sleep. Repeat.

The only change was the landscape around us. Trees and shrubs were gradually losing the battle to rocks and dust. By the third day, we were trudging through a barren landscape. A few knee-high shrubs could be seen here and there, between volcanic boulders just big enough to sit comfortably on. Ironically, it was the only day we would encounter rain on our hike. It started as a gentle drizzle that made us wonder if it warranted an additional waterproof layer. When it turned into a respectable downpour, we hastily stopped to put on our parkas. Our guides, on the other hand, took out the umbrellas hanging from their bags above their shoulders. Daudi stood out the most, in the best way possible, with his bright pink umbrella against the dark volcano.

We spent the morning crossing the Shira Plateau. Lahara explained that the plateau was actually a caldera—another fancy name to say that there used to be a volcano here, and then it erupted, gave its all, and finally collapsed, forming this large depression. The wide-open ground displayed deep valleys and weather-beaten lava flows. It made us realize how expansive

Kilimanjaro was and how many tracks we could follow. But we knew where we were going as, straight in front of us, the summit stood proudly.

To my left, Younes was recording a video. It sounded like he was talking to his girls, describing this uncanny landscape. Porters started passing us effortlessly, and I watched out for our group, looking forward to the friendly greetings and encouragements. It felt great to have a team around. Now and then, I overheard some of Younes's words. "… When you train a little, you can reach small goals. When you train a lot, you can reach huge goals …"

As we walked past a *Senecio kilimanjari*—an endemic tree that can only be found on Kilimanjaro, and that looks like a couple of huge, blackened pineapples liked each other so much, they decided to share the same trunk—my thoughts got fuzzy. Not because of the otherworldly-looking trees surrounding us. I recognized the feeling right away. It was how it had started on Aconcagua. I was at the onset of suffering from altitude sickness.

Just as I was finally about to get rid of my flu-induced headaches, they were going to be replaced with altitude-induced ones. The end of the pain had been in sight. And of course, I miraculously put myself in a situation that would extend my despair.

I tried to remember what ailment would come next but got stopped in my tracks by Rama, who left the trail in front of me and took out his notebook. I remembered Rama mentioning, "I am an engineer just to pay the bills, but who I am at my core is an artist; that's my whole identity." Curiosity took over, and I followed him in the shrubs to look over his shoulder.

He was drawing in meticulous detail a rocky protuberance. I looked up, but everywhere my eyes landed, I could only see the same barren landscape. Nothing stood out. It was all the same. The same views we had seen all day.

"Are you drawing something in particular on the mountain, or just rendering what this landscape looks like?" I finally asked.

Rama pointed far away, toward the horizon. "There. Do you see it?" I seesawed between Rama's drawing and the faraway mountain, long enough that I wondered if I should just lie and say yes to put an end to this awkward search. When I was on the verge of lying, my eyes locked on something. The flawless replica of Rama's drawing. Against an ordinary drop, a huge bulge stood out. It was so easy to miss. So easy to think that it was all the same. Rama reminded me of a quote by Einstein: "There are only two ways to live your life. One as though nothing is a miracle. The other as though everything is a miracle." Rama had chosen to see miracles and beauty all around him.

Kilimanjaro was beauty.

We must have been above 14,000 feet because all alarm signals were flashing red in my body. My stomach was unsettled, and I kept wondering if I should throw up. My head was hurting just enough to be an ever-present bother but not enough to warrant mentioning it to others. Walking became an annoying motion.

I suffered in silence until we stopped for lunch at Lava Tower, at around 15,000 feet above sea level. The blue tent had been set up at the top of a ridge, and food was ready for us. Everyone welcomed the break, and lively conversations started all around me as everyone helped themselves to yet another delicious soup. In my corner, I pushed my chair back and put my head between my hands.

"You need to eat a little, Florian," Daudi said. I forced myself to look up and offered a smile that I knew didn't quite reach my eyes.

"I am getting ready for it! I just need a little moment," I answered. He nodded and left the tent.

After a few minutes, the cheerfulness in the tent became oppressive. Didn't they know that we were supposed to feel awful and talk about turning around? I sprang up and left. I walked aimlessly, not looking at where I was going, and got lost between the tents of other groups until I reached the edge of the improvised campground. I slumped down and resumed my resigned position, sitting on the ground.

A porter I did not recognize came to me. He was not from our group. Another helping hand I need to turn away, I thought. "Food?" he asked, bringing his hand to his mouth. It took me a moment to realize he was not telling me that I should eat. I had heard of companies that didn't feed their porters enough. I was hoping it was not true. But this man left little to the imagination. He was hungry. Behind him, I could see a small group of porters huddling and waiting expectantly for the scene to unfold. I considered going back to my group's tent to pick up food for all of them, but I could not find the strength to get up. I felt horrible. I just could not move. I apologized sincerely and buried my head once again.

I don't know how long I was there or how he found me, but Daudi suddenly materialized next to me. "We are ready to go down to camp. Are you ready?"

I thought about his question. "As ready as I will ever be. Let's do this."

"Did you eat a little?"

I shook my head no, too distressed to answer out loud. I remembered the hungry porters and looked around in case Daudi could help get them food, but they were nowhere to be seen.

"Make sure to eat tonight. Your body needs it, regardless of how you are feeling."

I nodded, and we joined the group to start the 1,600-foot hike down to Barranco Camp. I was hoping that, just like on Aconcagua, going down in altitude would quickly heal my broken body, but I did not seem to improve. On one of the rare occasions when I looked up from the ground in front of me, I saw Fred running frantically down the steep volcanic slope. Thomas was right behind him, following effortlessly.

"He says he is tired, but I think he is suffering from altitude sickness. He decided to run down to Barranco Camp and nap," I heard a voice explain.

I felt bad, knowing that Fred was probably suffering the same pain I was, but his reaction did not make sense to me. I too was tired. I too wanted to nap. And I was contemplating thousands of options to improve my wellbeing, but running down to camp had not crossed my mind and would not make it onto the list. Fred was really cut from a different cloth. Amid the pain, he had revealed yet another beautiful lesson about why we were here. Yes, we were walking as part of a group. Yes, we had guides and porters. But when it came down to it, we were alone. Alone to know how we felt. Alone to decide what we needed to do.

Kilimanjaro was facing our distress alone.

And so I kept on trudging. Alone.

When I reached my tent, a porter met me to help take off my boots. I thought about politely refusing, but I was too glad for the help. I took off my left boot while he took off the right one.

"What is your name?" I asked.

"Dastan," he answered, smiling.

"Great meeting you, Dastan. Thank you for the help. I am Florian." He nodded as if he wanted to engage in a conversation, but stayed quiet. I realized that he did not speak English, and I did not speak Swahili.

After a quick nap that barely helped alleviate the pain, we all met in the blue tent. I couldn't eat, but I still moved a carrot and a potato covered in sauce from the main plate in the middle of the table to my own plate. I moved them around to make it look like a lot of food had been sitting there. I even nibbled on the carrot when Daudi walked in.

We started our health routine, passing the oximeter around until Rama stopped our smooth flow. He was looking at his results, dubious. After five long seconds, he snapped back into reality and attached the oximeter to another finger for another reading. He looked like he had either come to terms with the decay of his forefinger and wanted to check on the fate of his other fingers, or he had decided that all of a sudden, his forefinger wasn't compatible with the oximeter, and he was determined to get an accurate reading. The new reading seemed to have the same effect on him as the first one.

"I am at 89 percent," he announced reluctantly.

"How are you feeling?" Lahara asked.

"Good. Same as the days before."

"Then it's OK for now. Let's see how you are doing tomorrow."

My oxygen levels were still in the nineties, but I felt horrible. The group was still ranking at 9 or above. I felt peer-pressured and chose to be an 8.5, to convey that it was not a walk in the park for me. It was way higher than what my body was telling me I was, but I did not want to stand out too much, in fear of eliciting concern or sympathetic conversation that would only drain me more, as I would feel the need to reassure everyone.

When I walked out of the dining tent, the mountain looked the same, but this little finger-squeezing device had lifted the veil and revealed the truth: the air was thinning, and our bodies were starting to struggle to find the oxygen molecules they desperately needed.

KISS THE ROCK

The only part of the hike that required some rock-climbing skills was the Barranco wall, our challenge on the fourth day. After leaving camp, we zigzagged through a field of huge moss-covered boulders until we reached the bottom of the vertical 800-foot rock wall. The wall was irregular enough that it was often easy to find holes and bulges to use as steps and handholds. At times, the "steps" into the rock were just deep enough to fit the front half of our boots, but, with our porters and guides providing guidance on what positions and footholds were best, we were able to navigate even the trickiest sections. I now understood why Paul thought that hikers on Kilimanjaro needed to be sure-footed. A fall here promised a handful of broken bones and could even be deadly.

On all fours, looking for ways to climb up, keeping an eye on everyone in the group to make sure we were all safe, and vividly aware of the constant danger of this sheer trail, I was happily surprised to feel excitement. This was fun. I felt like a kid again, climbing a wall, jumping from rock to rock.

We made our way up quite slowly, everyone opting for safety over performance. Porters were flowing around us, finding ways up the rock face that I could have sworn did not exist moments earlier—at least not for humans. The porters not only made mountain goats' best tricks look trivial, but they did so while balancing heavy bags on their heads and backs. Keeping their balance should have been impossible. Yet none of them fell or even slowed down.

"I really don't know how they do that. They are doing so much for us," commented Younes when we got stuck in traffic before Kiss the Rock, a particularly narrow section that Lahara had warned us about the night before. "Alfred, the porter who carries and sets up my tent, was even trying to help me take my shoes off yesterday. I guess I looked like I needed it," he continued.

"Yeah, I was offered help too," I answered. Ashamed to confess I really did need help out of my boots, I quickly changed topics. "Are you scared of Kiss the Rock?" I asked, pointing my chin at the line in front of us.

Kiss the Rock was a section of the wall where the only way forward was a narrow edge, six feet long and two feet wide. Hikers had to face the wall, arms spread on each side for balance, and walk sideways before stepping on a large flat rock. This edge earned its name, as it looked like the people on it were hugging and kissing the rock face. A cute name for a section of the wall where a fall meant certain death.

"No, I am good with heights," Younes answered. "But this guy doesn't look very assured."

I took hold of a large crack in the wall and leaned over the edge to look ahead. A hiker from another group was on the narrow edge, trailing his hands along the wall. He looked over the side to the boulder fields several hundred feet below, immediately stopped in his tracks, and his face went back to kissing the rock. After a long and passionate hug, he resumed his small side steps, toward the safety of the large platform.

Less than an hour later, we reached the top of the Barranco wall. My adrenaline level dropped. My inner child, who had had so much fun rock climbing, retreated. Once again, I was a mundane, headache-ridden hiker battling altitude sickness. We crossed over a scree to descend into the green Karanga Valley, where we set up camp. Once again, I had no appetite. I went to bed exhausted, cold, and feeling weak. Altitude sickness was winning the battle.

CAN'T HIDE ANYMORE

On day five, the climb started to become a mental challenge in addition to a physical one. My legs felt good enough; they weren't asking for a break or a slower pace. The troublemaker was my brain, constantly screaming in pain because of a headache that seemed to usurp all of the energy in my body. The message was clear: "STOP CLIMBING UP, YOU IDIOT! You were born by the sea. You belong at sea level." The feeling was quite disarming. I knew that stopping would not help. I knew that continuing forward would not help. My only option for a quick relief was to turn around, which was not a thought I was ready to entertain just yet. So here I was. Feeling trapped. Every second was a fight.

"There is nowhere else to go. Just make it to Barafu Camp. You'll be alright, eventually" was the thought on repeat in my head. Barafu Camp was located at the foot of the summit cone. It was our last camp before attempting the climb to the summit.

My only relief came from reminding myself that, on this launching pad to the summit, a nap full of healing promises awaited. I tried to avoid the thought that Barafu Camp was at an altitude above 15,000 feet.

At some point along the way, even thinking became too

complicated. Every time a thought materialized, the pain barged in and shoved the thought down, leaving me confused and with a primal desire for it all to stop.

My field of view included my feet, the dusty gravel that formed a lifeless path, the sharp, dark volcanic rocks of various sizes scattered randomly alongside the trail, the occasional knee-high shrub, and the feet of the person in front of me. This became my world. I only focused on matching the speed and direction of the feet in front of me. The dusty gravel path was always the same, always going up with a doomed certainty.

"We're going to take a break at the top." Daudi pointed ahead, where the path disappeared over a rocky hill into the blue horizon. I had no idea how long we had been walking or how long was left, but stopping sounded like a bad idea. I would be left alone with the pain and no feet to mindlessly guide me.

The top of the hill revealed more dusty path, going down on the other side into a shallow valley before climbing back up into a large rock formation. "Barafu Camp is right behind these big rocks. We're almost there! Let's take a five-minute break."

I took off my day pack and lay down in the dirt, arms and legs spread out, with my hat over my face, and without a care in the world for appearances. I wondered if I could take a five-minute nap, but nausea came knocking and had other plans in store for me. I battled discomfort until finally Lahara asked us to get ready. I got up and realized that everyone had taken their break on their feet and was ready to go. I put my pack back on and joined the line. That was the moment my stomach decided it needed some attention from the group. I turned around just in time to throw up on a shrub instead of the trail or a fellow hiker. After three noisy projectile streams of light yellow bile, I felt confident enough to straighten up and get back in line. Everyone was staring at me.

"What are you all waiting for?" I asked in my most innocent tone. Resorting to humor has always been how I diffuse tension.

I was feeling weaker than I ever had on the trail, and the concerned looks I was seeing in everyone's eyes probably meant that my pale face was betraying how I felt. After a few awkward seconds, the column turned forward and started walking down the valley.

Younes slowed down to get to my level. "Doing good over there?"

"Never felt better," I answered, my way of saying I was not well, but I believed I would survive. There was no hiding that I was suffering from acute mountain sickness anymore.

The final push down and back up the valley was a grueling exercise, blurred by the pain. The sour taste of bile in my mouth was vivid enough to be a conspicuous companion.

By the time our team made it up the other side of the valley, I was ready to close my eyes and never open them again. I asked Younes to check in for me at the Barafu Camp office, and Dastan, who had welcomed us at the camp entrance, walked me to my tent.

Barafu Camp was by far the busiest of all the campsites we had been to. All the different routes up Kilimanjaro converged here. Several streams of hikers who would be attempting the summit tonight were flowing into the camp that already looked full. At 15,100 feet, Barafu Camp was also the highest camp on the mountain. It was the same altitude as Lava Tower, where I was so sick I hadn't been able to eat anything. At this altitude, there was barely any vegetation. Everything around us was dark gray rock.

It quickly became obvious that Barafu was also the least camp-friendly of all the campsites. The terrain was uneven, and the "path" through camp required some rock-climbing acrobatics. Considering this torn scene, the number of tents that had found enough flat gravel to stand on was quite impressive. We kept walking down toward the lower levels of the layered camp, further and further away from the summit. As always when I unjustifiably saw myself as a victim of unthinkably cruel suffering, I decided that now was the perfect time to wish the world were a more compassionate and equitable place. Why were the first groups that arrived, which were clearly composed of happily frolicking hikers, setting up camp on the prime higher layers of Barafu Camp, closer to the summit? Surely, going down an additional couple of hundred meters was nothing to them. Meanwhile, here I was, wondering what would be less painful: trudging down the rugged path or hurling my body over the rocks, hoping that I'd land on a tent to cushion my fall.

I set aside all thoughts of making the world a better place and of throwing myself off the mountain once the porter pointed to our camp. The tents were crammed together to fit in the small, flat area between a huge rock and a hundred-foot vertical cliff. Here and there, human-sized volcanic boulders had fallen on the campsite. Between the tents and the deadly fall was the permanent bathroom, sitting precariously on the edge. It had two doors, but was so close to the void that I didn't know if the doors opened on toilets or hurled you all the way down. At least the view was incredible. From this large ledge, we had an unobstructed view of the barren landscape below the snows of the summit. Everywhere we looked was gray dust spread on dark rocks among the clouds.

"I am going to take a power nap. Do you know when the debrief with the guides is?" I asked Ashim, who was busy around camp.

"As soon as they are done checking in. Maybe ten minutes?"

"Perfect, that's nine minutes and forty-five seconds' worth

of sleep."

I crawled into my tent and quickly fell asleep in my dirty clothes.

"Florian," said my tent, shaking, with Daudi's voice. "We're meeting now."

I had no idea if I had slept ten minutes or two hours. I put on my flip-flops (it was too cold for them, but I didn't have it in me to tie shoes) and headed to the dining tent, where the debrief was underway.

"… discussed among ourselves, we feel it's better for Team Chapati to start the summit climb at 10:30 p.m. tonight," said Lahara. I looked at my phone. It was 6:10 p.m. "That's earlier than most groups," Lahara continued, "but given our pace, it is best for us to leave early." Yet another injustice. The slower groups arrived late, only to be told that they wouldn't have much sleep because they had to leave early. I stopped fuming once I realized I was probably a major reason why the whole team wouldn't get much rest. I felt horrible. "Any questions?"

"Is there any fun hike to do around here before 10:30 p.m.?" I deadpanned in an effort to lighten the mood.

Lahara gave a hint of a smile. "Even if you're not tired, we recommend lying down to be ready for the twelve-hour hike to the summit and back. It will get difficult for everyone." He nodded toward Daudi and Thomas. "Even for us." He paused long enough for everyone to listen intently. "But tomorrow, remember: pain is temporary; pride is forever." He could have sounded cheesy, but he did not.

In our silence, Daudi stepped in with our health trackers. "Let's take our measurements and then get some rest."

I was feeling like a 4 when I managed to forget the headache and how weak my body was, and like a 2 when I didn't. How high could I rank myself without looking like a complete fraud? I settled on a squirmy 7 and was forced to check the "vomiting" and "lack of appetite" boxes because of my public displays. Tomorrow's push to the summit and the hike back down couldn't come fast enough. I wouldn't be able to keep up a brave facade much longer.

Once the team was done measuring oxygen levels, our guides reviewed the results and debriefed in Swahili before turning back to us.

"Everyone can attempt the hike to the summit tomorrow. Except you, Florian," Lahara said, turning toward me. The words were followed by a heavy, palpable silence. I looked around the room, confused, looking for an answer. All eyes were on me, showing a mix of surprise, sadness, pity, and some relief.

"I have to try at least. I don't feel that bad," was all I could mutter.

"You said you were a 7. It's too low."

Well, at least I had kept my 2 and 4 hidden, or I would be rushed downhill in a stretcher. "It was a temporary 7 because I just threw up. Ask me again in ten minutes, and I'll be a rising 8, jumping up and down with excitement!" My face managed to produce a large smile that I hoped conveyed a confidence that didn't exist.

Lahara's eyes narrowed. "Are you sure you are an 8?"

I stopped longer than I should have. I still didn't know how to assess how bad my acute mountain sickness was and how dangerous the push to the summit really was. I would later realize that, given my constant and intense discomfort, I was truly putting my life at risk. But in front of everyone, for no acceptable reason, I decided that there was no time to think. "Positive. And 8 is my favorite number. How could I not be an 8?" I realized too late that joking while they were trying to assess whether or not I was walking to my death was not my best move. "I am an 8. I am confident I can try to summit," I lied.

Lahara paused to think. "Alright, let's reassess in three hours before we depart," he finally said. He only seemed half-convinced. That was good enough for now.

I headed back to my tent, determined to sleep every last second I could. Sleep had been the only effective medicine on the mountain. I hoped that three hours would be enough for my restorative functions to work their magic. But it was hard to be optimistic: I had the worst headache yet, my body felt very weak since throwing up, and the rising heat in the tent took away any hope for quality sleep. Lying down, alone, I finally paused to wonder if Lahara was right about putting an end to this adventure. The pain was so overwhelming that I could not tell myself that everything would be alright anymore. My body was reaching its limit. The realization hit hard: I had limitations; blind optimism can only take you so far. Maybe I had run away from my burnout as far as I possibly could. Maybe this was as far up the mountain as I was supposed to climb. It was hard to know, with this throbbing headache that prevented me from thinking straight. At this point, it felt like whether I'd see the summit or not was out of my hands and was up to my headache. What was up to me was if I should even risk trying.

In my despair, I remembered the note Celeste had written. I had completely forgotten about it and was now four days late in opening it. I ransacked my bag, took out the letter, and started reading.

"Florian, you're here! You made it! You rose up against all odds to be here, on Mt. Kilimanjaro. I am so proud of you. I know your days are long and tiring, but remember that Clarke and I are thinking of you each step of the way, sending you the strength and the power to carry on."

That was my answer. I knew that Celeste had not been picturing me feeling so poorly when she wrote the letter, but it was the first time that my unborn daughter was sending me strength and power. I could not let her down. I would go to sleep, wake up, make it to the summit, and run the hell back down.

A SILENT DEPARTURE

9:45 p.m. Wake up in a flash, adrenaline pumping. Turn off the alarm clock. Take a quick scan of head and body. No headache, no drowsiness from the lack of sleep. First win on summit day. I started breathing again.

I tried not to think about the strenuous undertaking ahead and decided to take it one step at a time. For the first time in five days, I put on clean clothes, but anxiety prevented me from appreciating the moment. I went out and over to the dining tent. The whole team was already there, eating "breakfast."

"Hi, everyone! Ready to do this?!" I said in my most cheerful tone. These were the words my typical self would say. I tried to smile, but I was sure they could tell I was anxious. On the other hand, they all seemed confident and ready to go.

I wondered if, to them, I looked confident and ready to go, while they were trying to hide their anxiety.

Five minutes later, Lahara, Daudi, and Thomas walked in. I had only been able to eat a couple of crackers, as my body was still punishing me for bringing it to such a high altitude.

"How is everyone feeling?" Lahara asked. All three of them scanned the room, and one by one, we all confirmed that we would be attempting the climb to the summit. "Here is the order we'll walk in: I'll go first, followed by Rama, Florian, Fred, and then the rest of you." It was hard not to associate this marching order with who they thought would be the slowest or the first to give up. Rama had been falling behind the last few days. I was severely weakened, unsure of when the pain and discomfort would be too much. And Fred had been experiencing mild altitude sickness. Meanwhile, everyone else—Fiona, Younes, Hughes, Raoul—had shown no sign of distress whatsoever. Lahara had made a humbling but logical decision.

I felt a knot in my stomach. I had thought I would have more time before climbing. I wanted more time. *First do; then think.* I usually used my familiar catchphrase to make a spontaneous decision and move on with a risky option. For maybe the first time ever, I realized that today, I would need to use my catchphrase for a full day, as I'd need to keep pushing myself for over eight hours up a mountain instead of just making a quick decision in the moment.

But there was more. My catchphrase sounded different today because I was not mindlessly making a rash decision. I was looking at the situation square in the eyes. I knew that I was at risk and might not make it to the top. And yet my body had brought me up here, and it was worth pushing through discomfort to see the summit. Not because I had anything to prove, to others or to myself, but because the challenge was worth it. Kilimanjaro was worth it.

One task at a time. Fill up water bottles. Lace shoes. Put on day pack. Turn on headlamp. Go meet the group waiting to depart. Take a deep breath and smile. *First do; then think.*

Next thing I knew, under a sea of stars scarcely hidden by clouds, the group began walking without fanfare, and I picked up the pace behind Rama.

We walked through the dark, quiet camp in silence, as most

of the other groups would continue sleeping for at least another hour. My headlamp illuminated just enough space for me to see Rama's feet in front of me and the width of the narrow trail. This fuzzy halo became the whole world I focused on; everything else was pitch-black. I enjoyed the silence as I concentrated on my breath, making a conscious effort not to waste energy talking.

Once we left the camp behind us, the path became increasingly steep and rocky. The first hour went by fairly quickly. When we stopped for a brief water break, I happily noticed that my head hadn't begun to throb in unbearable pain yet.

But my joy was short-lived. As we started walking again, I could tell that I was not as clear-minded as I should have been. I suddenly became aware that no matter how deep my breaths were, I never seemed to take in enough oxygen to be fully satisfied, as if the air were noticeably thinning and we could suffocate at any moment. Once again, I tried to shut out the world and focus on my halo of light and my breathing, instead of overthinking how bad the headaches would get. I would know soon enough.

I lost track of time but was brought back to reality when someone at the back of the line asked the group to stop. I turned around and saw Fred sitting down, holding his head with both hands. Everyone started gathering around him: the team, the guides, the two porters, and Gabi. Not a good sign. I stayed ahead of the trail for a bit, thinking that we would start walking again soon. Going back down even twenty feet seemed like a significant effort. Plus, my head had just started spinning, and I didn't want to announce it to the group.

Five minutes went by before I realized that this wasn't just a quick break. I walked down to meet the group and saw tears on

Fred's face. The knot in my stomach came back threefold. I knew his physical pain. I had felt it acutely the past couple of days. The headaches. The nausea. The general feeling of being sick without being able to pinpoint what was wrong. The body screaming for it all to stop. But I was even more devastated, thinking of the psychological pain he must have been suffering—after traveling across the world and spending five days hiking, this was the end of the path for him. He would not see the summit.

I couldn't think about what to say to comfort him. In an impulse, I walked up to him, put my hands on his shoulders, and clutched harder than must have been comfortable. He was still looking down. I sent him whatever energy I had and walked back up in front of the group, before the option of giving up became too real.

Soon after, Fred was helped up by a porter and Thomas. The three of them started walking back down toward camp. If Fred, a world-renowned athlete, couldn't make it, what hope was there for me? I would at least go as far as I possibly could.

In that moment, all pride abandoned me, and I took off my day pack.

"Daudi, do you think someone could help carry my day pack?" I asked, trying not to sound alarmed.

"Yes, give it to me." I now understood why he and Thomas hadn't brought their own backpacks. They knew some of us would need help. Well, the Southern French guy was the first one to give in.

As the group started walking again, I felt lighter, but my head wasn't improving.

Just make it as far as you can. First do; then think.

ANY THOUGHT?

"How are you doing, man?" Younes was right behind me, and I could tell that he was purposely trying not to speak to me too much, seeing that I was quieter and more focused than usual. But the caring leader in him could not help but ask.

"Light-headed, but so far so good; no unbearable headaches. Thanks." He was not even out of breath, so I decided not to ask him how he was doing. This guy was built for physical challenges. I would ask him later. When I felt better.

Another hour went by before the next break. I slumped down against a boulder and closed my eyes. While I didn't experience the throbbing headache from the previous days, I was increasingly light-headed, and I could tell that I was not thinking clearly. We were at 17,500 feet, the highest we had been so far. I knew that, when the headache came, it would be legendary. Fred's face was still unsettlingly fresh in my mind.

"We are going to form two groups," Lahara announced. "I'll stay behind with Rama, and we will walk slower. Another group will go faster with Daudi."

I could feel all eyes turn to me. It was obvious that Younes, Fiona, Hughes, and Raoul would go with Daudi and enjoy a faster pace. My first thought was that I shouldn't slow them down. But before I could finish this thought, it was chased by a much more vivid one: "If you stay behind, you will never make it to the top. The headache will catch up."

Before I was able to assess the situation, my body took over. I jumped to my feet, went right behind Daudi, and said, "Let's do this! See you at the top, Rama!"

I did not know if the group was disappointed. I did not know if Lahara and Daudi hesitated or considered changing my mind. I did not know if anyone thought that I could make it. I didn't think I could. But I would make it as far as I could. No regrets.

No one said anything, and Daudi started walking. Fast. Much faster than before. After a couple of steps, I was completely winded. Objectively, we were not walking fast. At this pace on a flat surface at sea level, it would be considered a stroll. At an altitude of 17,500 feet, every step took its toll. It was a strange feeling. Physically, no muscle was hurting, and I didn't feel out of stamina. But my body was still screaming to turn around, or at the very least to stop walking, just to catch a breath.

After what seemed like an eternity but must have been closer to fifteen minutes, Daudi asked the group how the pace was.

"I am loving it!"

"Freeing!"

"Great!"

I did not answer. No need to complain; I had brought this on myself.

One task at a time. One step at a time.

And then I lost my balance. I did not fall, and the group behind me may not even have noticed it. As I straightened myself, I could tell that it wasn't exhaustion but light-headedness that had caused me to wobble. I tried to focus, as the path was still steep and precarious, but I couldn't. It was all foggy.

I wondered if there was a chance I could die. My default

mindset kicked in: dying was for old people. I knew I couldn't die because, first, I had to meet my baby girl, and second, the youth in me still whispered that I was indestructible. I agreed ... at first. But being pushed so far out of my comfort zone gave me perspective. I knew that I was heavily biased toward accepting and welcoming risk. I couldn't rely on my gut feeling, so I started running through scenarios. If I fell and started rolling down the mountain, I was not sure that my body had the strength to handle the shocks. If I passed out, porters could probably carry me down. But how to know if I could be brought down fast enough to escape the most serious symptoms of altitude sickness? I had no past experiences to compare; I didn't know how my body would react at this altitude and under duress. I didn't know what was causing my light- headedness and how serious it already was.

For a moment, it felt like there was just me and a raw, wild volcano. Here, life hung by a thread. It was overwhelming, and I started panicking. I couldn't do this. As I felt my willpower melt, something that I had never experienced happened. I started seeing and feeling my wife and my unborn child send me strength. The strength they had promised me. I started sensing Younes, Fiona, Hughes, Raoul, and the whole Chapati team encouraging me. I started hearing my mom and sister telling me I was inspiring them to make ambitious changes in their lives. I started visualizing my dad looking up and seeing the same sky as the one above me on his birthday. For the first time of my life, I was persevering thanks to the strength of others instead of mine. It felt powerful, and I could feel tears forming.

One step at a time. One step at a time.

I startled. *You are falling asleep!* I could not believe it. I was supposed to be full of adrenaline, wide awake under the effort. But no, my body was shutting down.

I stopped walking. The group stopped behind me. Daudi noticed after a couple more steps and turned around.

I didn't speak, but I trusted that my face delivered the message. I was done.

"Do it. Do it." Daudi didn't ask any questions. He didn't want to know if I had a headache. If I was about to puke. He wasn't even encouraging me. He was telling me. I did not have a choice. As my body started moving again, before I could decide if I wanted to turn around or not, I realized that Daudi was what I had learned to call a "quiet leader." He wasn't the most extroverted person, but he carried an aura that commanded respect, and when he was focused on you, you listened. You listened because you instinctively believed in his decision-making, in his strength, and most of all in his integrity.

The group followed. And we walked again. And again. I wobbled again. I started falling asleep again. I focused only on the next step. It seemed like we had been walking for another eternity. I wanted to give up with every step. I was not finding the usual "challenge accepted" energy I dig into when faced with difficulties. There was just the next step.

Note to self: never, ever do any other activity that involves walking. Especially not in hiking boots.

The weariness grew. Until I stopped again. I could not remember why I had started this journey. I could not remember why it was worth it. I just knew I had to stop walking.

The group stopped behind me. Daudi noticed.

"Do it." I hesitated. And moved forward again. It was just easier to be told what to do instead of forming my own thoughts.

Later, when I was down from this dreaded and loved volcano, I would wonder what I had lost as my body was shutting down, and what had opened to cause me to delegate my decision-making so easily.

But all this came later. On the path to the summit, my all-consuming thought was survival.

Daudi turned to the group. "Move over to the right of the trail," he instructed us. I looked up and saw three people rushing down the narrow trail. Something was wrong. They were going way too fast on these treacherous, slippery rocks. As they got closer, I realized that a hiker was being held up by two porters. The hiker was a man in his fifties. The porters were half carrying him. His face and eyes didn't seem to register what was happening around him. No one asked if he was alright. If the porters were risking a dangerous fall by running this fast, the hiker must have been suffering from more than just acute mountain sickness. I forced myself to remember the other, more serious types of altitude sickness. Pulmonary edema, when fluid builds up in the lungs. And cerebral edema, when fluid builds up in the brain. Both were life-threatening. As the trio rushed past me, I could have sworn that the catatonic hiker turned his head toward me, as if to make sure that I kept in mind which symptoms were coming for me next.

First do; then think.

After walking for yet another eternity, Daudi stopped and pointed to a sign 200 feet ahead of us.

"This is Stella Point. It's easy after that."

WHAT IS LEFT

5:28 a.m. Our group made it to the top of the steep wall. A large wooden sign to the right of the trail said, "Congratulations, you are now at Stella Point, 5,756 M / 18,885 Ft." I heard hearty congratulations and enthusiastic encouragements coming from behind. The team joined the line of hikers waiting to take a celebratory picture in front of the sign. I was in no shape to celebrate. I decided instead to trudge to the left of the trail and slumped down on a large boulder. Maybe I'd join them once they were at the front of the line. In the meantime, I'd hold my head with both hands.

"Are you OK, Florian?" Daudi asked. I hadn't heard him get close. I realized that I must have looked exactly like Fred did, just moments before he had to turn around.

I forced myself to look up but couldn't muster a reassuring smile. I was fighting tears of exhaustion. "I think I have nothing left."

Daudi turned to the group. "Let's take pictures on the way down. We keep going."

There it was. The group was sacrificing for me once again. I should have stayed behind with Rama and Lahara. But no one complained, or even hesitated. They broke away from the line to join Daudi and me. Shame forced me up.

"Let's go. It's easy now," Daudi repeated as he started walking at an infernal pace.

This time, something felt different. My feet made a squeaking noise with every step. The path was wide enough for two or three people to walk side by side. It was almost flat, and everything around us was white. A new kind of cold lifted my chin up. Snow. We were walking on snow. How did I not notice the snow? This realization pulled me out of my misery loop long enough to allow me to take a deep breath. Fresh air flowed down my throat and filled my lungs. It felt invigorating.

The scene all around us was magnificent. Tucked inside a frozen half-pipe, the path went on forever into the clouds. On each side of the frozen half-pipe were stunning glaciers. The sun was announcing its upcoming rise by painting some clouds pink against the deep, dark blue sky. My core and my limbs felt increasingly sturdier and stronger.

I gave a hint of a smile and turned to Younes. "Breathtaking, isn't it?" I commented.

"Yes, what a sight!"

"How are you doing?"

"Doing good, but for the first time since we started the hike, I can feel the burn." He pointed his chin toward the rest of the group behind us. "It's hard for everyone. You're doing great."

I disliked needing to be reassured. But it felt so good to know. I faced forward once again and enjoyed this moment of sharp awareness. I observed the few clouds in what was otherwise the promise of a bright blue sky in the morning. I noticed the snow on the path was hard, frozen, as if it had been here forever. The whole volcano looked frozen from here. Kilimanjaro was showing us a brand-new face, its most powerful yet. Despite the cool breeze, the air was not as cold as the still landscape would suggest. Ironically, as Kilimanjaro put on its winter jacket, I started feeling warmer.

It was fitting that the last push to the summit was a bit slippery. It forced even the most tired hikers, and those on the verge of being nonresponsive like me, to be fully present and focused on the path.

"Daudi," Younes called from behind me, "can someone also help with my backpack?"

"Yes, give it to me," Daudi answered.

"But you already have one."

"It's OK. Give it to me."

Younes hesitated but ultimately complied. Daudi put the new backpack on one shoulder and kept walking without showing any trace of slowing down.

"I feel like I can fly!" Younes vigorously moved his arms up and down as he ran a couple of steps to experience his newfound freedom. I remembered that his day pack was much heavier than mine. I didn't know how he had carried it this far, but I could imagine his relief, which brought me right back into my own body. Weariness. There was just weariness. I was drained. I focused on my breath again.

More white. More wind.

In front of us, the sun was now a fuzzy ball of brightness in the dusty white horizon.

Now and then, Daudi glanced back, but the whole team was covering good ground. My brain jolted. I wondered if my light-headedness was finally morphing into a headache. If I wondered, it probably meant that it was. I tried not to think about it.

"We're almost there!" Daudi announced.

I looked up. More white. Some wind. I looked back down and focused on walking. One step at a time.

I heard whispers. I felt excitement all around me. I looked up again. And I saw it. The wooden sign of Uhuru Peak. I recognized it from all the pictures. I could see the summit.

I felt my body walking toward the wooden sign on its own. My mind went elsewhere. I was trying to understand what this meant, what I was supposed to think, what I was supposed to do, what I was supposed to feel.

My face tickled; something was dripping down. I was crying. As soon as I realized it, I started sobbing even more.

I felt empty. I had left all my energy, all my willpower, and all my pride way down the mountain. Here and now, there was no way to cover. No need to cover. I was crying because I had battled Kili for five days, skirmish after skirmish, and we were now nearing the end of the fight. I was crying because Kili had opened up and was trusting me with its summit. I was crying because I had not made it here on my own. My wife, my daughter, my family, and the whole Team Chapati had brought me up here, and I wanted them to feel what I felt.

I had given Kili everything. I was crying because I had nothing left but tears, and now Kili was demanding even these as I reached its summit.

Was it joy I felt?

A hundred feet to go. Younes had caught up with me. We made eye contact, but neither of us spoke. Words couldn't do justice to what I saw in his teary eyes and what he saw in my drenched face.

6:18 a.m. Uhuru Peak. We were at the top of Kilimanjaro.

I suddenly remembered why I had chosen this date for summit day. I looked up to the sky, and I saw the sun piercing the horizon. This was the sun of February 7, 2020.

Happy birthday, Dad, from the roof of Africa. We made it.

KNEES ARE OVERRATED

Fiona, Hughes, Raoul, Younes, and I regrouped and joined the short line of people waiting for their must-have photo in front of the summit sign. Under the proud flag of Tanzania, the sign read, "Mount Kilimanjaro. Congratulations, you are now at Uhuru Peak, Tanzania. 5,895 M / 19,341 Ft. AMSL. Africa's highest point. World's highest freestanding mountain. One of the world's largest volcanoes. World heritage and wonder of Africa."

To me, Kilimanjaro now held all of these titles and more.

After taking the picture that immortalized our humbling effort and our presence among the clouds, I scanned what was left of my body and mind. I definitely had a headache. And it was increasingly making itself known. The quick break at the summit had done wonders, though. I could feel traces of energy coming back to me. I might make it down on my own two feet.

"Is everyone ready to go?" asked Daudi. I definitely was.

"Already? Can we have five minutes to take it in? We've walked for five days just to be here," replied Raoul.

"Alright, five minutes."

Raoul and Hughes looked for a flat spot to sit down. Raoul ransacked his backpack and took out a flask. "Whiskey, anyone?"

This man was a genius. He had prepared for Kilimanjaro with an acclimation climb on Mount Meru, he was organized enough to bring a flask of whiskey to the top of the mountain, and he was bringing celebrations to the next level. I wished I had thought about and done all of these things, but, in stark contrast, I had elected to show up utterly unprepared. The consequences were now due in full; no celebratory whiskey for me. Who knew what havoc it would wreak in my shell of a body?

I engraved this scene in my mind.

Climbing Mount Kilimanjaro was a celebration.

Nearby, Gabi was chatting with a porter. They were both wearing sneakers and what looked like puffy, old sweatpants. It took me a moment to realize that they must be wearing several layers of pants so that the thin layers would add up to something comfortable at this altitude. Gabi's outer layer was a bright turquoise fleece jacket, which looked like a luxury item compared to the ragged jacket the porter was wearing. Neither of them had gloves. Gabi had a balaclava; the porter didn't. I felt a bit ashamed in my well-insulated clothing. To make matters worse, I remembered that the huge bag Gabi was carrying was filled with items we might need. Despite the cold and the weight, Gabi was still smiling. Of course.

Five minutes passed, and we started the not-so-fun walk back to camp. My head was now properly throbbing. It was not the debilitating pain I had experienced when I had thrown up or during lunch the day prior, but it was getting there. At this point, I was just hoping that I would get back down quickly enough to avoid the most serious symptoms the rushed-down dead-eye hiker had displayed.

Halfway down the frozen half-pipe, we heard a familiar

voice.

"Hi, everyone!" Rama's expression oscillated between the surprise and joy of seeing us. "Did you make it to the top?"

"We did! You're almost there."

"It's OK," answered Rama, "I was content once we made it to Stella Point. The sun rose just as we reached the snow, and I knew then that this moment was the reason why I came to Kilimanjaro. I was ready to turn around, but Lahara insisted that I also see the summit, so I'm here for him."

This was a perfect example of who Rama was: content in the present, with no need for glory, but performing miracles to make others happy. If he didn't exist, someone would have to invent such a human being. Right then, Rama reminded me of Alex Caruso, a Lakers player who looks like your next-door neighbor on a basketball court but dunks over seven-footers, regularly shocking everyone watching. The words I remembered from a commentator came out of my mouth. "Rama the machine. You cannot stop him. You can only hope to contain him."

We all wished him good luck and moved on. At Stella Point, we took the team picture we had failed to take a couple of hours earlier. I rallied and smiled for the picture, despite being close to the point of hurling my guts out on the frozen path.

That was the last act of heroism left in me. "Daudi, I need to go down fast," I pleaded. "The inside of my brain is aggressively pushing against my skull. I'm afraid it's trying to escape."

"I've got bad knees, so I won't be able to go down faster," Raoul said.

"Me neither; going faster doesn't look safe on the scree," added Fiona.

I looked at the scree over the edge and got their point. In broad daylight, it was clear that we were about to engage on the long and very steep descent on gravel that could give way at any time. It didn't look safe at any speed.

I looked back at Daudi. "I'll go ahead of the group, and I'll stop if I get lost or if it gets too dangerous, but I really need to get down quickly." With these reassuring words of wisdom, I started jogging down the precarious path. After a couple of steps, my feet slid, and I started skiing down the scree. Fear and adrenaline kicked in, enough for me to stay up until I slowed down and came to a halt. Instead of taking Kili's warning seriously, I made two executive decisions. First, I would never put on these shoes ever again, so I could keep using them as skis until they were ruined. Second, healthy knees were overrated. I started moving again and went down in a random mix of frantic run, uncontrolled drift, and everything in between. For the first time this week, the fear of falling and getting legitimately hurt felt real and imminent. Falling here was not like falling upright on the way up. Falling here meant falling awkwardly, potentially head first, with little hope of slowing down my fall. But I was even more afraid of my headache getting worse. I kept going.

I was making good ground, albeit looking like a drunkard trying to stay straight on a skateboard. The sound of rocks rolling under my feet was exhilarating. Until I looked down. Every one of my steps was starting a small avalanche of sharp volcanic rocks. Luckily, the path was cutting across the scree to the right, while my avalanches were claimed by gravity straight down. I hadn't killed anyone. Yet.

I started sweating heavily. I hadn't realized that the sun was now rising in a cloudless sky and was quickly heating up this infernal, windless hill of dark rocks. I hadn't realized that I was dying of thirst either. And at about the same time, I remembered that Daudi was still carrying my bag with all my water in it. Great, if my knees didn't fail, hurling me down a 3,000-foot fall, dehydration would probably claim me.

I slowed down and came to a stop, to catch my breath and take off my jacket.

"Everything good?" asked a voice behind me.

I turned to find Gabi—you guessed it, smiling—standing right next to me. He didn't look tired, and, more importantly, he didn't seem to be judging my questionable downhill technique.

"I'm doing fantastic, Gabi. I didn't hear you. You'll have to teach me the art of flying over gravel someday." This was the best bad joke I could come up with to take his focus away from my erratic breathing.

"Give me your jacket. There is room in my bag." I was too grateful to argue. He took off his bag, and stuffed my jacket in.

"Thanks, Gabi. Ready?" I asked, more of myself than of him.

"Ready."

I resumed my chaotic slide while Gabi somehow managed to run gracefully. After a time, the path flattened enough to warrant walking. The camp was close.

AN UNSUSPECTED SURPRISE

By mid-morning, we entered a quiet Barafu Camp. With hikers out trudging to the summit, the porters were enjoying some well-earned slow time, sitting in circles and laughing and resting. Dastan and a couple of other porters were chatting at the edge of the camp, keeping an eye out for hikers coming back. When he saw Gabi and me, Dastan surged forward to inquire about our adventures, and Gabi debriefed him in Swahili. Dastan handed me a pineapple juice box, and I insisted that we split it three ways. I was clearly the one who needed the energy and hydration the most, but this was a time to bond and celebrate.

Trudging through the camp, I marveled at the resiliency of the human body: after laboring for nine grueling hours up to the summit, and with seemingly nothing left in the tank, we had miraculously made it down in a couple of hours.

"Welcome back!" Thomas greeted us as we got to our campsite. He turned to me. "Did you make it to the summit?"

"I did! It was truly incredible."

"You did?!" he let out in disbelief. There was no insult, just a genuine conviction that I should never have made it to the top. He quickly recovered. "Congratulations, my friend!"

Thomas, thank you so much for keeping your experienced reservation to yourself until now.

"How's Fred doing?" I asked.

"He'll be OK. He is resting in his tent."

"Great. I'm going to copy his strategy. Do you mind waking me up when we need to get ready? I'm afraid that, if left unchecked, my body will pass out for forty-eight hours uninterrupted."

"Will do, my friend. You should have a couple of hours before we head out to Mweka Camp. Congratulations once again."

I went to lie down, but sleep evaded me. My headache constantly pulled me back to the world of the flesh. My mind was still racing, busy recounting over and over again the events of the last twelve hours in random order. I still didn't know how I was supposed to feel or what today meant to me.

I was in a sleeplike state when the camp started singing. The singing morphed into loud, celebratory screams. I stumbled out of the tent just in time to see the whole Team Chapati—all the porters, William, Ashim, Gabi—form a tight crowd that Hughes, Raoul, Fiona, and Younes were slowly walking through, triumphant. A chaotic myriad of high fives was being distributed along the slow procession. Ashim hugged Younes with so much energy that both his feet left the ground. Genuine exhilaration was palpable.

One by one, I also congratulated Hughes, Raoul, Fiona, and Younes. As our eyes met, the feelings of pride and shared accomplishment were overwhelming. I had never felt closer to them all. They all had the same look on their faces. A look that said, "I made it." Their tired faces were four versions of the same fulfilled smile.

After checking in on each other, we scattered around camp

to rest and start packing.

"I'm happy to see that you look a bit tired," I told Younes. "You're human after all."

"Ever since the summit, I've felt exhausted. I think my mind was blocking any pain or thoughts of pain until I made it to the top, because there was no way I would fail my girls. But now the floodgates of weariness are open." He smiled. "Can't wait to sleep tonight."

"Story of my life on Kilimanjaro!" I said sheepishly.

We parted ways, but the feeling of celebration didn't leave. I noticed that I had a smile on my face. Not a forced one for once. The fight was over, and, for the first time since we started this adventure, I went to my tent not to sleep but to relax and listen to music.

An hour later, Rama and Lahara entered the camp and were greeted with a similar enthusiasm. Rama looked the same as always, with a quiet force that could keep him going at his own pace forever. He humbly accepted the praise and congratulations from everyone.

"We leave in thirty minutes," Lahara announced.

The sun was now high in the sky, making our tents unbearably hot and leaving us with two equally unappealing options: roasting on our comfortable mattresses or resting on sharp volcanic rocks, hoping for the occasional cold breeze. I felt deep in my bones the conviction that humans were not meant to live here, or even be comfortable here. Temperatures seemed to purposely stay outside of the range acceptable for humans. At night, it was freezing, and the only way to be comfortable outside was to move. During the day, the high altitude and the proximity to the equator meant that the temperature rose quickly, and UV radiations were a lot more harmful than at sea level.

When we finally departed, I looked back at the summit, with a renewed respect for this extreme place on Earth. Uhuru Peak looked exactly the same as the first time I saw it, days earlier. And at the same time, looking at it made me feel something completely different. It was the type of feeling that cannot be put into words. The type of awe mixed with intimacy that needs to be experienced rather than recounted. One thing was for sure: I would never forget this day.

THE DAY AFTER

The hike down proved relatively easy after the arduous push to the summit. My leg muscles were finally sore, but gravity was a consistent, helpful friend. Along the way, vegetation reclaimed its dominance. Rocks and dust became shrubs. Shrubs became scattered small trees, which then became thick tree groves lining the path. And finally, we reached the rain forest again, back to where we had started a week ago. As I sank deeper among the green, towering trees, my head started to clear.

We were all tired when we reached Mweka Camp, our final camp on the mountain. Despite the exhaustion, our last evening together was filled with heartfelt celebrations. All our senses and our awareness were heightened by the bittersweet knowledge that it was the last time dancing together, singing together, eating together. It turned out that Fiona was born on the same day as my father, and a porter coming from Moshi had brought a birthday cake up to our last camp.

After dinner, the whole team brought the cake to the dining tent to sing "Happy Birthday." It was the first time that all thirty-one of us were in the tent. Crammed in together, singing, there were no porters, no guides, no tourists, just a group of human beings who had been forming bonds for a week and were now celebrating together as equals. It all felt so natural. Fiona cut the cake in the smallest slices possible so that everyone could have a bite.

Then came yet another celebration, the "tipping ceremony," in which the team pooled a tip for the group and Lahara translated in Swahili the amount everyone was getting. Lahara insisted that we all say a few words afterwards. When Fiona shared that her family and friends would think that she was crazy for going on a strenuous weeklong adventure in a remote environment and as the only female in a group of over thirty people, I realized how disconnected I had been to the experience of others this week. I had been so concerned with my physical ailments that I hadn't even noticed Fiona was the sole woman in our group.

I had always enjoyed public speaking—telling a story, making people laugh, sharing inspiring thoughts. When my turn came, I tried to explain how life-changing this experience had been for me and describe the role that each and every person around me had played, but the words that came out of my mouth did not quite fit. How to describe how majestic Kilimanjaro was? How to describe the storm of emotions that I had felt these past twenty-four hours? As I looked around the circle, I had to cut my speech short; it got too long and too emotional for my little heart. At the end, as we all slowly drifted away, I found Dastan and gave him the remaining cash I was carrying. Tipping him was a very small token of appreciation, given everything he had done for me this week, but it felt like a good start.

At the exit of the Kilimanjaro National Park, Thomas was waiting for us with a last gift: a local banana beer. A last wink for all the amazing uses the Chaga had for this abundant fruit. The ride back to Moshi was quiet. The same old bus that had brought us to Machame Gate was now driving us away. The only difference was that, after six days in the wild, the seats now felt unfathomably comfortable.

Rocked side to side by the road winding down the lower slopes of Kili, feeling safe in the seat that had adopted my body shape and was now hugging me, I was trying hard not to fall asleep; I wanted to catch every last glimpse of the surroundings passing by. The banana trees were still there. The one-story, flat-roofed Chaga houses with their colorful doors and windows were still there. The wide dirt sidewalk blended seamlessly into green grass, and then got lost in thick green bushes and green trees. I could have sworn I saw the exact same dog I had seen before, walking across the same portion of road. Life had both kept on going and stayed still at the same time. The only thing that changed was what I was feeling. What had been an exciting window into a new and exotic culture on the way up was now a vision that commanded a solemn reverence. These banana trees were part of Kili's ecosystem. The Chaga people were the guardians of this formidable giant. They knew Kili more intimately than I ever would. Five days was a drop in their ocean of knowledge and experience. It was almost insulting to say that I had conquered Kili. Especially considering in what shape I was dragging myself by the end.

The ride back was also quiet because all of us knew that this was the end of our adventure. This was the ride back to "real life," whatever that meant. Most of us were flying back home the next day, just to go back to work the following day. Had the rest of the world also stayed still?

After a quick stop at the headquarters to drop off our rented gear, we said our goodbyes to Lahara, Thomas, and Daudi. These three men, along with the whole team of porters and cooks and aides, had made it possible for us, outsiders, to peek into one of the most astonishing treasures of Tanzania.

Back at the same hotel I had stayed in the first two nights, we were greeted with cautious smiles that turned into warm congratulations once we confirmed we had made it to the top.

"Would anyone like to have their hiking boots cleaned?" asked the receptionist.

All my energy was directed toward making it to a shower and bed before my legs gave way under me. Having clean boots was about as low on my priority list as could be, but it seemed an appropriate closure to get help a final time with my boots. A last hand to clean off any remaining trace of hardship. I handed them off, as did the whole team.

It was time for goodbyes. With Fiona, Rama, Younes, Fred, Raoul, and Hughes in this concrete building, doing something administrative like checking in at a hotel felt out of place. Our team had only been together in the wild. Team Chapati belonged in the wild. In this dimly lit lobby, the reality of the finality of our journey together hit hard. We promised to stay in touch. We hugged. We shook hands. And after a last look at each other, we headed our separate ways.

I picked up my keys, was told that my room was on the second floor, and started the long, slow walk toward my resting place. I stopped at the bottom of the swirling stairs outside to take in the moment. The afternoon sun was warm on my face. Laughter came from people playing in the swimming pool. The suffering was finally over. Everything was going to be alright.

As I took my first step up, my legs mutated. What had been perfectly functional muscle tissue for thirty years now felt like heavy concrete blocks, with needles sticking out and threatening to pierce my skin if I dared to continue moving upstairs. Soon, my solid legs were refusing to contract and stretch—necessary activities for anyone ambitious enough to engage in the complex act of walking. I stopped on the second stair, and, ashamed that a swimmer might be watching and wondering what was wrong with me, I pretended to listen to the birds singing in the trees above while I evaluated my options.

After trying different ways to move my treacherous limbs, I settled on a swaying stiff-legged approach that I hoped would leave me looking somewhat normal as I made it to the top. First, I would sway my upper body to the left, keeping my legs as straight as possible, and then use kinetic energy to slingshot my right leg onto the next stair. Finally, I would laboriously drag my backpack up and repeat the process with the left leg.

After several draining minutes, adorned with the most relieving swears I knew, I was safe and sound on the second floor. There was no way I would be going down these stairs for dinner tonight. I silently thanked the universe for making me so sick that I still had some chocolate bars in my bag.

Walking down the outside corridor was the employee, dressed in brown, who had just dropped my boots off and disappeared down another flight of stairs. So much had happened while I was swaying up the stairs. I kept trudging toward my room and made a mental note to tell the management to book ground-floor rooms for tired hikers, and keep the stairs for freshly arrived travelers oblivious to the pain to come.

Once inside my room, I dropped my bag and clothing to the ground, picked up my last clean pair of underwear, and wobbled to the shower. After five days of superficial cleaning in the freezing hours of the morning, my body screamed with joy when I stepped into the hot stream of water. The heat flowing down my skin brought life back into my sore muscles, one by one. The regular, familiar sound of water hitting the tiles relaxed my mind. The smell of shampoo was overwhelming and made me realize that my brain had blocked off any sense of smell these past days. Probably in an attempt to keep me from passing out from my own hard-earned sweat.

Manifesting a strength I did not know I had, I managed to extricate my body from the shower before emptying Moshi's water reserve. I migrated to the spacious single bed and picked up where I had left off before my nature retreat—yes, I mean I picked up my phone. Eizaguirre Land had been suspiciously quiet since my last message. I reread it with fresh eyes and was hit by the lethal connotation. "Hopefully I'll message back in seven days!" Oops.

I called Celeste and shared that not only was I still alive but that I had also made it to the top. "It was a life-changing experience," I added. "I am so glad I was able to be part of it, but I will never, ever hike again in my life." I would say this last bit to everyone I spoke to in the next few days, convinced that it was the truth. Little did I know, hiking would soon become a go-to pastime.

After hearty congratulations, Celeste confessed that she and my family had been a bit stressed this week.

I apologized for leaving them concerned and followed up with a call to my sister, to take the pulse of the situation at home. "I think that Celeste put it mildly," was my sister's feedback. "Mom and Dad barely said two words to each other on Dad's birthday because we were so worried about the summit hike."

Her words made me realize that once again, I had heard but not listened. But now that it was all over, I could see clearly. I could see the sick obstinacy of youth that had pushed me to come here unprepared, regardless of the dangers that others had seen from the start. I could see how I had run away from a burnout that was only a symptom of a much larger issue. Having felt something truly powerful reminded me that I wanted my life to be more. More meaningful. More impactful. Kilimanjaro had not given me the answer to what my life should be about, but it gave me a new mindset to get started. There was no shame in needing to go through a long physical conditioning before braving the highest freestanding mountain in the world. There was no shame in needing help. I had learned that I had limits, and that turning a blind eye to them was not going to make them go away.

I had learned that I couldn't always first do, and then think.

A NEW WORLD

Seven Months Later—September 2020

The world has changed. For two reasons.

First, because of a global health crisis. Borders are closed. To travel means to expose ourselves and others to a virus we don't know enough about yet. We are all confined at home with no end in sight.

The second reason is scarier. And infinitely more powerful. Her name is Clarke. She is a couple of weeks old. She doesn't know it yet, but I made it to the top of Kilimanjaro thanks to her. One day, I will tell her the story. But not now. Now, I am learning to become a father. Clarke is teaching me. She started with patience. Most of the time, nothing is urgent to a newborn. Nothing needs to be rushed. I am learning to be comfortable living fully in the present, doing nothing but looking at her.

Clarke starts every day with a big smile. It is the first thing she does when she wakes up, without fail. She does not seem to need a reason. She just wakes up and smiles. Celeste and I are learning to do the same.

My parents and sister had to cancel their trip to the US to meet Clarke, as Europeans are not allowed in the country. And

I cannot go back to France. It is strange not to be able to return to my home country, but still, I do not feel trapped.

I feel like my quest for meaning has ended. Where there used to be a desperate desire to escape as far away as possible, there is now a strong belief that I am exactly where I am supposed to be. I feel guilty for being happy while the rest of the world is struggling. I cannot imagine what mental state I would be in if the pandemic had come seven months earlier, when I was lost and burned-out.

Celeste noticed the change. She asked me why I do not feel the need to travel anymore. Why I am not speaking every other day about potential trips around the globe. Why I am not asking her if she would be open to moving permanently to New Zealand. Looking at Clarke sleeping on my chest, the best answer I can offer her is "I didn't know I already had everything I needed here."

I am still processing my experience on Kilimanjaro. I am left with strong emotions attached to snapshot memories. I think of how I was humbled in the best possible way. How I was exposed so much that I cannot lie to myself anymore about my limitations. When stripped of everything, the real self has nothing to prove. Not because pride disappears, but because there is no point in being anyone other than who we are.

The words of Lahara often come back to me and still ring true. "Pain is temporary. Pride is forever." The pain is gone. And I am proud.

My quest for meaning has ended. At least for now.

ACKNOWLEDGEMENTS

Writing this book has been an experience unlike any other. Some words came out as planned. Some were hard to write. Some surprised me. From the moment I started writing to the time this book was published, I gave up a thousand times. Some very special people helped me pick up my fountain pen again.

First and foremost, Celeste. Everything I do is tainted by your creative genius. This book is no exception. Thank you for your brutally honest feedback and for all the advice on how to improve. And of course, thank you for the book cover!

This book would look very different without my editor, Marcia Trahan. Thank you for helping me look deep inside to make this book the best it could be. Working with you has been a great source of joy.

Mike, you were the first person (outside of myself) who believed that this book would see the light of day. I often think of your confident words of encouragement, shared right before we jumped headfirst over the giant Connect 4 at John's wedding. They made all the difference when it got hard. Thank you.

Thank you to everyone who read bits and pieces of this book and provided helpful feedback: Barb, Paula, Marion, Taylor, Rana, Ryan, and Daryl.

And last but not least, thank you to the whole Team Chapati. I would not have made it without you.